ISEE Lower Level Exam Prep

2020-2021

ISEE Study Guide with 512 Test Questions and Answer Explanations (4 Full Practice Tests)

Table of Contents

Chapter 1: Introduction to the ISEE Exam

The Independent School Entrance Exam (ISEE) is for students in the fourth through 11th grades who wish to gain entry into grades five through 12. There is also a separate exam for second and third graders applying to independent schools. The ISEE exam is generally taken because a student wishes to be accepted into a private school which requires the ISEE as part of their admissions process.

There are three levels of the ISEE. These are the Lower Level exam, the Middle Level exam and the Upper Level exam. The Lower Level exam is specifically for students who are currently in the fourth and fifth grades and who are trying to gain admission to a private school for grades five and six. For the purposes of this study guide, we will be going over the information, requirements, rules and study materials that are needed for the ISEE Lower Level Exam.

The ISEE is administered as part of the admissions process nationally for most private schools. The verbal reasoning, quantitative reasoning, reading comprehension and mathematics sections all include questions with multiple-choice answers. The scores for these four sections are made available to the school you are applying to, along with your essay. The essay is not scored as part of the exam but is sent to your intended school for review with the rest of your scores.

Gaining admission into private schools is generally an extensive process and schools take advantage of the ISEE to standardize at least part of the process. By doing so they can evaluate everyone applying to their schools for the same grade with one specific measure of prospective students' academic skills, abilities and academic retention.

Regardless of the level of the ISEE test you will be taking, the exam is composed of five sections. All five sections are grade-level appropriate.

The Verbal Reasoning & Quantitative Reasoning portions are designed to measure your reasoning abilities and focus on skill more than the amount of studying you cram in before your exam. Reading Comprehension and Mathematics Achievement sections are designed to measure how you answer reading and math concepts, the retention you've maintained throughout your schooling and the things you should know at your grade level.

Finally the Essay section provides a grade-level appropriate topic for you to write about. It tests your overall ability to organize your thoughts and write a well-thought-out, detailed, clear essay.

ISEE Registration, Fees and Testing Locations

The ISEE exams are administered in three different settings: large group, small group and independent testing settings. Testing either takes place in a school that is a member of the Educational Records Bureau, an ERB testing center or at a Prometric testing center. The Education Records Bureau oversees the ISEE.

Schools are usually used for large-group settings, especially when a large school is having its own individual enrollment season. Some schools arrange for all of the students applying to their school to test on a set day and time. That said, ERB-associated schools also do large-group testing strictly for all students, regardless of where they wish to attend.

Testing centers and Prometric testing facilities are generally used for small-group testing or for those students who choose to test independently. Prometric is a private company that facilitates a wide range of tests for an array of fields, and the ISEE is just one such test.

Parents register their children for the ISEE. Once registered, you will receive a letter in the mail that will confirm your registration, your test date, time and location. That letter will allow your student entrance into the exam on testing day. Registration can be done online at erblearn.org or by calling 1- 800-446-0302. The ERB website is a great resource for additional registration information and can provide help with rescheduling or canceling as necessary. For those planning to test at a Prometric facility, registration is online at iseeonline.org.

ISEE Testing Fees

Large-Group Testing – Online Registration	$125.00
LATE Online Registration – Large-Group Testing	**$155.00**
Large-Group Testing – Phone Registration	$150.00
LATE Phone Registration – Large-Group Testing	**$180.00**
Small-Group Testing – Online Registration	$195.00
LATE Online Registration – Small-Group Testing	**$225.00**
Small-Group Testing – Phone Registration	$220
LATE Phone Registration – Small-Group Testing	**$250.00**
Individual Testing	$225.00
WALK-IN REGISTRATION (Only available at some locations) **Special Requirements Apply	ADDITIONAL $40.00 and the registration MUST be processed online
Prometric Testing Center Registration	$200.00

Testing Retake Costs:

Large-Group Setting	$110.00
Small-Group Setting	$180.00
Individual Test Setting	$210.00
Prometric Testing Center	$190.00

ISEE Rescheduling Fees

- There is a $35 rescheduling fee for small- and large-group testing. You can reschedule up to 24 hours before your exam.
- You will FORFEIT your registration fee if you cancel less than 24 hours before your exam or if you miss it entirely.

ISEE Cancelation Fees

- If you cancel up to 24 hours before the exam, $45 will be deducted from your registration fee and the remainder of your money will be returned to you.
- There is **NO REFUND** if your cancelation took place more than 90 days after you originally registered, if you cancel less than 24 hours before your scheduled exam or if you miss the exam entirely.

Prometric Testing Facility Rescheduling and Cancelation Policies

- You can reschedule up to 15 days before your exam at no additional fee.
- You can also cancel your exam completely up to 15 days before the test and receive a full refund.
- If you reschedule 15 days before your exam there is a $30 rescheduling fee.
- If you reschedule up to 24 hours before your exam there is a $75 rescheduling fee.
- If you cancel 5 to 14 days before the exam, $30 will be deducted from the registration fee and the remainder of your money will then be remitted to you.
- If you cancel 5 days or less before the exam you will receive no refund.
- There is also no refund if you miss the exam completely and you will be required to pay a new registration fee if you wish to register for the exam again.

Waiver Program

For those students whose families may have trouble meeting the fees associated with the ISEE, there is a waiver program offered. Parents must contact the school they are testing for and apply for the waiver through them. The family must meet the financial need requirements in order to qualify for the waiver program and all required support documents must be submitted with the application in order to be considered for a waiver.

Unless arrangements are made through your institution, waivers must be approved before you register for the exam.

Testing & Testing Day

There are three testing seasons for the ISEE:
- The fall testing season, which runs August-November.
- The winter season, which runs December-March.
- Finally, the spring and summer testing season, which is one testing season rather than two, and runs from April-July.

While the ERB discourages students from testing more than once in a 12-month cycle, students are allowed to test once per testing season. This ultimately allows students to test up to three times in a 12-month testing cycle.

All of the levels of the ISEE are made up of the same five sections. Each level has questions that are specific to particular grade levels. The exams are made up of (1) Verbal Reasoning, (2) Quantitative Reasoning, (3) Reading Comprehension, (4) Mathematics Achievement and (5) an essay question.

The five parts of the ISEE are all timed. For the ISEE Lower Level Exam there are:

- 34 questions in the Verbal Reasoning section that must be answered in 20 minutes.
- 38 questions in the Quantitative Reasoning section that must be completed in 35 minutes.
- 25 questions in the Reading Comprehension section that must be completed in 25 minutes.
- 30 questions in the Mathematics Achievement section that must be answered in 30 minutes.
- The essay section that requires you to brainstorm on a given topic, put together a brief outline and write a thorough essay in 30 minutes.

The total time allotted for the exam is 2 hours and 20 minutes. When the time for one section has concluded, you will not be allowed to return to that section. Any unused time will not roll over into the next test section.

There are two breaks provided during the exam. Once you have completed the Verbal Reasoning and Quantitative Reasoning portions, the testing instructor will generally allow students their first 10-15-minute break. During that time you will not be allowed to leave the testing facility premises, but you can get up, move around, stretch, use the facilities and get a drink. Once the break is over, the exam will resume and you will complete the Reading Comprehension and Mathematical Achievement portions. Then the testing instructor will generally give you your second 10-15-minute break. Once your final break has concluded you will complete the final section of the exam, the essay.

The first four sections of the exam will be scored by the testing facility, while the essay section will not receive a score. The test results will be released to the school(s) you are applying to, with a copy of your essay. When the scores have been tabulated they will be uploaded to a private server, and an email will be sent to parents informing them that scores are ready for their review.

The scores will be released to the parents of the student via an online parent portal. While the scores will be available on the ERB website, a hard copy of the exam results can also be sent to parents for an additional fee. Note that the scores will not include a copy of the essay for parents.

The ISEE Exam Scores will only be released to the parents and schools which you have specified should receive a copy of your scores Any additional schools you wish to allow access to the scores will need to be added in writing by notifying the testing facility. This is done to ensure the confidentiality of your information and scores.

Testing Format

The ISEE exams are administered in one of two ways. The exams can be administered via paper and pencil or online. The format will depend on a few things, including your group size and the testing location.

On test day, you will need to bring with you:

1. The verification letter you received by mail after the registration for your exam was complete
2. Student identification – types of acceptable ID include:
   a. Birth certificate
   b. Social security card
   c. School ID
   d. Report card
3. Parent Identification (Prometric facilities require a government-issued ID)

For the paper and pencil exam you will also need to bring:

1. Four **sharpened** #2 pencils
2. Four hand-held erasers
3. Two ballpoint pens (either blue or black ink and they may be erasable, if you so choose)

Special Accommodations

For those who have a disability and need special accommodations in order to take the exam, the ERB offers a special accommodations application at https://www.erblearn.org/parents/isee-accommodations.

Accommodations cannot be provided until after an application has been successfully submitted and the accommodations have been approved. Thus, those needing accommodations should wait until their approval letter arrives before scheduling their exam.

Be aware that depending on the accommodations you require, you may be limited on the locations in which you can test.

Testing Rules

All students taking the exam must arrive no later than the time listed on their registration confirmation letter. No one will be allowed to take the test if they arrive late and/or if the test has already begun when they arrive.

Once the test begins, all students should manage their time well. Failing to manage your time well will affect your overall performance and the number of questions you are able to complete. While you don't want to run out of time, you should also not rush, which may lead to making mistakes.

Students are not allowed to bring anything with them except the items specifically required for the exam. Items you may not bring into the test center include (but are not limited to) cell phones, smartwatches, calculators, rulers, paper, books and any kinds of study materials.

Once everyone is seated for the exam the instructor will go over the rules and directions. Pay attention to your answer sheet and make sure your information is correct. Some testing facilities will fill out your personal information ahead of time to make the exam flow more smoothly.

Students should try to answer each question. Scores are only based on the CORRECT answers. Incorrect answers receive no negative scoring. Therefore, the more correct answers you get, the better you will do.

Students at the lower level are required to get fewer answers correct than those in the middle and upper levels. Students may use the blank spaces in their test booklets for scratch paper and will fill their answers in on the separate answer sheet provided. The answers must be marked using a #2 pencil to darken the circle with the student's letter choice for each of the multiple-choice answers.

Scoring

The ISEE isn't designed as a pass/fail exam. It's designed to evaluate a student's understanding of specific topics, assess grade-level knowledge, and measure a student's ability to retain information, think logically and organize and express his/her thoughts.

Students taking the ISEE Exam are scored on a percentage scale ranging from 1 to 99. The higher the percentage, the better the student's overall score.

The testing site will forward exam answer sheets and essays to the ISEE Operations office. Once there, each test will be scanned, and an Individual Student Report (ISR) will be generated for each student. The ISR can be more important to some schools than a student's GPA.

The ISR ONLY contains the scores for the four multiple-choice sections and does NOT include a copy of the student's essay. The ISR will be posted to the ERB family account created at the time of registration. As soon as the scores have been finalized through the scoring center, parents will receive an email informing them that they may view the scores at the ERB Member School website.

A hard copy of your scores can be ordered for an additional $25 fee and will be sent to you by mail.

About this ISEE Study Guide & Practice Tests

Welcome to your Independent School Entrance Exam Study Guide. This study guide has been specifically tailored for those taking the ISEE Lower-Level Exam.

This study guide includes information about the Verbal Reasoning, Quantitative Reasoning, Reading Comprehension, Mathematics Achievement and essay sections of the ISEE Lower Level Exam. It also includes additional information on the kinds of things you will need to know for the exam and some key study points to remember.

You will find four separate practice tests at the end of this study guide. In each practice test, there is a section on Verbal Reasoning, Quantitative Reasoning, Reading Comprehension, Mathematics Achievement and an essay question. All the test sections, except the essay, will include multiple-choice questions. The official exam will offer you two full lined pages to complete the essay. For the purposes of this study guide, use scratch paper or notebook paper to write your essay.

Following each of the practice tests, you will find an answer section with explanations include. Some of the more complicated questions will have more detailed explanations than others.

Chapter 2: Verbal Reasoning

Verbal Reasoning is your ability to use vocabulary. It is a skill that you expand and develop throughout your years of schooling and life experiences. Verbal Reasoning tests your ability to read a word, a string of words, a sentence, phrase or passage. It assesses your ability to analyze the meaning of the words, a phrase or the information you are presented with.

Verbal Reasoning skills are tested in a number of ways. You are verbally reasoning every time you are thinking about words or writing and reading. Any time you are considering written words, you may be doing one or more of the following:

- Thinking about the text you're reading.
- Solving a word problem in math class.
- Following the written instructions given in class.
- Reading the instructions for an art or science project.

While taking the ISEE Lower Level Exam, you will be required to draw conclusions about a word, story or phrase you are presented with. You may also be asked to determine what a sentence, statement or passage is implying or referring to when it's not stated plainly.

Below, you will find Key Study Points below that will help review some of the skills you may especially need to practice for the Verbal Reasoning part of the test.

Each test will offer you a variety of questions and four multiple-choice answers to choose from. The questions will be divided into **Synonym** and **Sentence Completion** sections.

Synonyms

In the Synonym section, you will be given a word. The word will appear in **CAPITAL** letters and will be grade-level appropriate. If you come across a word that you aren't familiar with, it is likely that there will still be a word or words in the answer options that you do know.

The word listed will offer you four multiple-choice answers—A, B, C or D—to choose from. The answer options are likely to help you eliminate at least some of the words and narrow down your answer.

Each of the multiple-choice answers will be a different word. The words given in the answer options will include at least one word that has a similar meaning to the **CAPITALIZED** word in the question.

You will use your verbal reasoning skills to:

- Think logically about the most sensible definition of the word you have been given.
- If you don't know the meaning of the word, try to eliminate the answers you know don't fit first.
- Consider the multiple-choice answers you have been given.
- Think carefully about the meaning of each word.
- Consider how the meaning of each word correlates to the **CAPITALIZED** word.
- Exclude words that you know have nothing in common with the **CAPITALIZED** word.
- Consider the words that may have similar meanings to the **CAPITALIZED** word.

Sentence Completion

In the Sentence Completion section, you will be given a sentence that is missing a word or words that are required to complete each sentence. You will need to ensure that the answer you choose makes sense and flows correctly with the portion of the sentence you were already given.

Just like in the synonym section, the multiple-choice answers will be listed as A, B, C and D. Using your verbal reasoning skills, you will:

- Carefully read each incomplete sentence.
- Carefully read each of the multiple-choice answers.
- Read the sentence silently, using each of the multiple-choice answers, one at a time, to see which one best completes the sentence.
- Eliminate the multiple-choice options that you know right away don't make sense.
- If there is more than one option that you think may fit, carefully read the sentence and those options over again to decide which answers fits the best.

Key Study Points for Verbal Reasoning

As a whole, the Verbal Reasoning practice tests will test your ability to:
- Recognize words and their meanings.
- Reasonably determine why one word or phrase most logically completes a sentence.
- Why the word you have been given is close in meaning or the same as the answer you have chosen.
- Problem-solve.
- Think logically.

- Find the right sequence of words that fit together in the most sensible way.
- Understand and follow directions.

Prefix	Examples	Suffix	Examples
de-	decrease	-able	retainable
dis-	disagree	-al	annual
ex-	explosion	-er	smaller
il-	illegal	-est	smallest
im-	impossible	-ful	fruitful
in-	intruder	-ible	invisible
mis-	misconduct	-ily	sleepily
non-	nonverbal	-ing	rushing
pre-	preauthorize	-less	listless
pro-	protest	-ly	surly
re-	remove	-ness	progressiveness
un-	undo	-y	messy

Synonyms

In this section of the exam, you will be presented with a series of questions that use synonyms to test your Verbal Reasoning skills.

Some of the ways you can practice the skills you will need to successfully navigate this section on the exam include:

- Review fifth and sixth-grade vocabulary words.
- Use vocabulary words in a sentence.
  - When it comes time for the official exam, using the **CAPITALIZED** word in a simple sentence will help you to find the correct synonym.

Take what you already know and apply that to answer the questions first:

- Does the assigned word have a **prefix** (the beginning of a word) or **suffix** (the end of a word) in common with any of the multiple-choice answers?
- Does the given word have a **root word**—a word that doesn't have a prefix or a suffix and belongs to a word family (i.e., *legal* is a root word that belongs to the family of words such as *illegal*, and *auto* is a root word that belongs to the family of words such as *automatic*.)
- Are there answers that you immediately know are wrong? Eliminate those first if there are.

Sentence Completion

In this section of the exam, you will be presented with a series of questions that offer an incomplete sentence and require you to choose the appropriate multiple-choice answer to finish the sentence correctly.

You will be presented with an incomplete sentence that requires you to complete it with a single word or multiple words. You will choose from the four multiple-choice answers to find the answer that most logically and grammatically completes each sentence.

One of the most strategic ways to choose the correct answer from the multiple-choice options is to follow these steps:

Step 1.   Carefully read the incomplete sentence.
Step 2.   Carefully read each of the multiple-choice answers.
Step 3.   Complete the sentence with each of the answer options. This will allow you to see which answer sounds correct and best completes the sentence grammatically.
Step 4.   If the answer isn't immediately obvious, there will be some multiple-choice answers that stand out as clearly wrong. Eliminate those.
Step 5.   If there is still more than one option you think might be correct, read over the sentence and answers again. There must be one answer that fits better than the rest.

Keep an eye out for transition words. These include:

- if
- then
- therefore
- also
- sometimes
- never
- not
- always

Words like these can help key you in on the right answers and guide you through picking out the words or phrases that simply don't fit.

Below is a list of fifth- and sixth-grade vocabulary words. Each word is accompanied by a definition of the word and/or a sample sentence. Review the list thoroughly and practice using the words you are less familiar with in sentences. Refresh your memory and get comfortable using these words and other words that you already know and which are close in meaning.

- abolish – to get rid of (I want to abolish the laws that make it illegal to walk backwards on Sundays.)

- absurd – ridiculous (It is absolutely absurd that I have to walk to school when it's closer to drive.)

- abuse – mistreat (The abuse that dog suffered was horrible, but now he will be spoiled and loved.)

- access – to gain entrance to (I have access to some highly classified buildings.)

- accomplish – to finish something (There are still so many things I would like to accomplish.)

- achievement – to complete something great (My greatest achievement was winning state with the rest of my team.)

- aggressive – forceful or threatening (The dog at the shelter seemed aggressive until I approached him and petted his soft head.)

- alternate – to switch back and forth between two or more different things (Mia and Anna alternate watering the plants and feeding the cats.)

- altitude – a height (Climbing to the top of Mount Zion took me to a whole new altitude.)

- antagonist – a person who stirs things up or exacerbates a situation (The villain in the story was a very believable antagonist.)

- antonym – the opposite of something (Pass is an antonym for fail.)

- anxious – excited and tense about something (The dog was anxious as he waited by the door for his owner to return.)

- apparent – clearly visible or obvious (It was apparent that my sister forgot to pick me up when she still hadn't arrived an hour after practice let out.)

- approximate – an estimated value or guess (I told my dad I would be home at approximately 9:00 p.m.)

- aroma – a pleasant smell (The fresh fruit and dark chocolate gave off a heavenly aroma.)

- assume – to make a decision about something without proof to support that decision (I can only assume that my sister took my new top since it's missing from my closet.)

- astound – shock or great surprise (I was astounded when my parents told us we were going to SeaWorld!)

- available – accessible, at one's disposal, unoccupied (The rooftop deck is available for my birthday bash.)

- avalanche – mass of snow and ice that falls very fast (I could see the avalanche from the resort on the other side of the mountain.)

- banquet – formal dinner for a large group of people (We are having a fundraising banquet on Friday.)

- beverage – a drink (My favorite beverage is Earl Grey tea.)

- bland – plain or boring (The steak I got at the restaurant was bland and rubbery.)

- blizzard – a strong snowstorm (The blizzard kept us snowed in for several days.)

- budge – won't move (I was so warm and cozy on the sofa, I didn't want to budge.)

- bungle – to mess up or make a mistake (I bungled my math test.)

- cautiously – carefully or with caution (I cautiously backed away from the mountain lion.)

- challenge – something difficult (I knew it would be a challenge to run the 10k race.)

- combine – to blend or put together (My chili combines an array of ground chicken, ground turkey and beans.)

- companion – to be a friend or confidant (Lisa is my closest companion on the soccer team.)

- crave – to want something badly (Every time the weather turns hot, I crave frozen watermelon slices.)

- compassion – to care or be kind to others (I hope that I can grow into a kind and compassionate person.)

- compensate – to give someone something in return for something they have done (I will compensate my buddy for watching my dog Lilly while I was out of town.)

- comply – to do what you are told or what is expected of you (We comply with the school's academic code so that we can play football.)

- compose – to put together in a neat and orderly fashion (I will compose myself before I walk on stage to accept my diploma.)

- concept – an idea (Certain math concepts can be difficult to grasp.)

- confident – to believe in yourself (Being on the cheer squad has made me a more confident young woman.)

- convert – to change something into something else (We used liquid nitrogen to convert our milk and sugar mix into handmade ice cream.)

- course – a class or lesson (The high school lets us choose two courses each semester as electives.)

- courteous – to be kind and polite (The visiting school was courteous when it came for the band concert.)

- debate – to disagree or argue a point (Vivian won the debate team rally this weekend.)

- decline – to turn down (I accepted an offer from Penn State so I had to decline offers from other schools.)

- dedicate – to devote a large amount of your time to something (I am dedicated to my role in this year's school play and can't wait for opening night.)

- deprive – to withhold or keep something away (I don't want to deprive my dogs of exercise so I take them to the indoor dog park whenever it is too cold to hike.)

- detect – to notice or pick up on (The computer won't detect my homework file, so I can't upload it to the teacher.)

- dictate – to rule over or hold dominion over others (My brother is dedicated to the lacrosse team and has never missed a practice or game, even when he had the flu.)

- document – an important paper (The DMV required me to bring two separate documents to prove my identity before I was allowed to get my driver's license.)

- duplicate – to copy or double (I made a duplicate house key to keep under a flower pot on the porch in case we get locked out.)

- edible – something you can eat (The fruit and chocolate arrangements our school sells for Valentine's Day are entirely edible.)

- endanger – to put something at great risk (We donate the proceeds of our basketball team fundraiser each March to the conservation of local endangered species.)

- escalate – to increase quickly (The fight escalated quickly and the whole thing was blown way out of proportion.)

- evade – to avoid or hide from (My mother fell asleep before I got home so I didn't have to evade her notice.)

- exasperate – to greatly irritate, annoy or frustrate (It's exasperating to come home every day and have to pick up my brother's things off the floor.)

- excavate – to dig out a hole (The city had to excavate a series of water pipes in town.)

- exert – to apply or influence (My big sister exerts herself running before bed; she says it helps her sleep better.)

- exhibit – to show off or display publicly (The school put on an art exhibit for all of the seniors in the art class this spring.)

- exult – to rise up in triumph or jubilation (I exulted when I received my acceptance letter to the college of my choice.

- feeble – weak, ill or sickly (My grandma may be feeble, but she shows up for my concerts anyway.)

- frigid – extremely cold (When the weather turns frigid, it's the perfect time for hot chocolate.)

- gigantic – extremely large (The mastiff at my friend's house is gigantic, but he thinks he is a lapdog and tries to curl up on you.)

- gorge – to eat huge quantities or a deep cavern (The kids at the high school lock-in gorged on pizza, candy and soda while watching movies on the projector.)

- guardian – a protector, someone who watches over others and protects them from danger or threats (The officer at our school is like a guardian angel.)

- hazy – not clear, fuzzy (When I got nailed in the head by a serve gone wrong during volleyball practice, everything was hazy for a little while afterwards.)

- hearty – strong, healthy and heartfelt (My mom makes a hearty meal for the whole baseball team the night before big games.)

- homonym – words that have the same pronunciation but different meanings (Bear, meaning a wild animal, and bear, meaning to endure something, are homonyms.)

- identical – exactly the same, without any differences, a duplicate (My sister and I are identical twins.)

- illuminate – to light up or brighten a space (The twinkle lights in the gym illuminated the space nicely for our homecoming dance.)

- immense – very large or taking up a lot of space (The auditorium was immense and also full of people.)

- impressive – awesome, grand, magnificent (The Grand Canyon is an impressive natural spectacle.)

- independent – to accomplish without requiring help or assistance (I completed my math homework independent of any assistance from my father.)

- industrious – hardworking and committed (The kid is industrious and runs his own lawn-care business in our neighborhood.)

- intense – strength, force or extreme (The basketball game tonight was more intense than usual since it was our rival team.)

- intercept – to get in the way of, stop, catch or cut off (Bobby was able to intercept the football and managed to gain the team an additional 10 yards in the process.)

- jubilation – with great joy and excitement (The students attended the graduation party with great jubilation.)

- retain – to hold onto or keep ownership of (I hope I can retain the information I studied for tomorrow's exam.)

- retire – to stop working, turn in for the night (My favorite teacher retired at the end of last year, but he still volunteers twice a week for a few hours.)

- revert – to return to or go back (The little boy, who recently learned good manners, has suddenly reverted to his previous bad behavior.)

- route – path on which you are traveling (The school bus takes the same route to and from school each day.)

- saunter – to walk in a slow and easy manner (If the hall monitors feel like there isn't enough pep in your step, they will tell you not to saunter, but to hurry up and get to class.)

- seldom – rarely, almost never, something that doesn't commonly happen (Seldom do I ever miss a day of school.)

- senseless – to be without thought, to act without thinking, to be careless in one's actions (It was a senseless decision to try to cross the street before the light was green.)

- soar – to rise (The bird soared above the mountain.)

- solitary – alone, to do alone, or to be on your own (Homeschooling can be a very solitary life.)

- solo – single, a performance by one person (I performed a solo in the school musical.)

- sparse – empty or bare (With four teenage brothers, the fridge is always sparse.)

- spurt – to gush out forcefully (When I squeezed the tube hard, the toothpaste spurted into the sink.)

- strategy – a plan or method to do something (The student's study strategy was to divide subject matters into chunks which he would study on different days of the week.)

- suffocate – to be unable to breath or be deprived of oxygen (If you climb a very high mountain without an oxygen tank, you risk suffocating.)

- summit – the highest point of a mountain (The cross-country team did a charity run to the summit of Mt. Glenn.)

- suspend – to stop, discontinue or end abruptly (I have never been suspended from school before.)

- synonym – a word or phrase that means exactly the same or close to the same thing as another word (Happy is a synonym for joyful.)

- talon – a claw, usually belonging to a predatory bird (The hawk has enormous talons it uses to catch prey with.)

- taunt – to tease, poke fun at or insult (It's poor sportsmanship to taunt the losing team.)

- thrifty – prudent, economical (I am thrifty, so I bought my prom dress at a vintage shop for half the price of a new one.)

- translate – to say in another language or express in a different form (The Korean student translated the visa application instructions for her parents.)

- tropical – very hot and humid, sweltering or sultry (Our science teacher keeps a tropical fish tank in the classroom.)

- visible – to be clearly seen (The track team wears reflective vests when they run in the morning to ensure they are visible to cars.)

- visual – to be able to see (It can be helpful to use visual aids when you are studying.)

- vivid – to be bright or eye-catching (The school got painted over summer break and the colors are no longer faded but are very vivid instead.)

- wilderness – out in nature (This summer our track team will be taking wilderness hikes as a team-building exercise with the new coach.)

- withdraw – closed off, kept separate from others, not social, keeping to yourself (After having her feelings hurt, the girl withdrew into her bedroom.)

- abandon – to desert, to stop caring for or looking after (The city looked deserted, but if you looked closely, you could see people behind the windows in the houses.)

- abundant – fruitful, plentiful, in large quantities (This year's fruit harvest was abundant because of the wonderful rain we received throughout the year.)

- access – a way of entering, the right to see someone or approach (Only people with certain credentials are allowed access to that top-secret room.)

- accommodate – to make adjustments (In order to accommodate three extra people in our house, we'll have to move furniture around.)

- accumulate – to gather or add up in one place (How have I accumulated so many books over the years, I don't know.)

- adapt – to make changes (I will adapt this backpack so it better fits me now that I'm taller.)

- adhere – to stick, cling, hold fast or attach to (The gluey substance adhered firmly to the wall, ensuring the poster stuck to it.)

- agony – pain (When the boy broke his leg on the football field, he was in agony.)

- allegiance – loyalty or commitment; fealty to a superior, group or cause (Each morning, we pledge our allegiance to the flag and to the United States of America.)

- ambition – the drive to be more successful (Joe has a huge ambition to become a physicist one day and knows he has to study hard to achieve his dream.)

- ample – a large amount, plenty, in great abundance (Mrs. Peterson has an ample supply of markers, which means other teachers borrow them frequently.)

- anguish – great suffering (There was a great deal of anguish in the hospital which the brand-new doctor visited.)

- anticipate – to expect something to happen, to prepare for the coming of something (The teenagers were filled with anticipation for the upcoming prom.)

- apparel – clothing (Each of the school's sports teams gets new apparel each season.)

- appeal – to make an urgent request (We appealed to the administration to hurriedly fix the leak in the middle school classroom, before furniture was further damaged.)

- apprehensive – anxious or fearful, uneasy (The young girl was apprehensive as she stepped into the kindergarten classroom for the first time.)

- arid – a dry, desert-like atmosphere (New Mexico has a very arid climate, which makes sense given how many days a year the desert state is sunny instead of rainy.)

- arrogant – self-important or opinionated; an exaggerated opinion of self-worth and value (Our quarterback is very arrogant and not a team player at all.)

- awe – a sense of wonder, amazement and astonishment (People sometimes stare at rainbows in total awe.)

- barren – failing to grow, flourish or produce (The barren lot is a terrible place to try and grow crops.)

- beacon – a guiding light, a marker, warning signal (Ships follow lighthouse beacons to safety during storms.)

- beneficial – good for, helpful, supporting (Some bugs can be beneficial to farmers.)

- blunder – a careless mistake, oversight or inaccuracy (Blunders are common; what's important is how you cope with them.)

- boisterous – noisy, energetic, cheerful (The boisterous boy ran down the hallway shouting at the top of his longs.)

- boycott – to cease the use or support of an item, person, group or cause (My mother has decided to boycott a certain store because she disagrees with how it treats employees.)

- burden – weighing down (That heavy backpack looks like an enormous burden.)

- campaign – offensive, advance, crusade (Kelly campaigned for vice president of student council at her high school.)

- capacity – the quantity which something can hold (The jar's capacity is one quart.)

- capital – city center, government hub, main point (Washington, D.C., is the United States' capital.)

- chronological – the order in which things happen (Reading things in chronological order is often easier than if events are out of sequence.)

- civic – local town and city duties and administration (It is every American's civic duty to vote.)

- clarity – clear view or revelation (After the rain, the sky seemed to hold a new, fresh clarity.)

- collaborate – to work on together (My science partner and I collaborate on our project together.)

- collide – to crash into something (I hurt my shoulder when I collided with another player during lacrosse.)

- commend – praise, congratulate, recommend (The principal commended the students for their outstanding grades.)

- commentary – narrative, report, account (TV reporters provide commentary as events unfold around them.)

- compact – small, fitting into a small space. (The middle school and junior high have full-size lockers but the high school uses more compact ones.)

- composure – appearance, state of mind (It can be hard to keep your composure when you're embarrassed.)

- concise – brief and to the point (My science teacher prefers clear, concise reports instead of many-paged documents.)

- consent – giving permission or agreeing to something (Adults must provide consent before teachers take kids on field trips.)

- consequence – the outcome of one's actions or choices (If you don't study for a test, the consequence will be bad grades.)

- conserve – to use wisely and with care (Our school has started a project to conserve resources and recycle.)

- conspicuous – standing out, being clear and visible (The dog was conspicuous walking around the middle of the classroom.)

- constant – always there, ever present (Constant practice is important to academic and athletic success.)

- contaminate – polluting or damaging (Too many car emissions can contaminate the air.)

- context – the circumstances surrounding an event (It's important to understand the context of a passage you are reading.)

- continuous – unbroken, whole, constant, continual (Continuous loud noise can get very tiring.)

- controversy – disagreement, dispute, argument (The referee's call at the ball game sparked a controversy.)

- convenient – suitable, fitting (Living close to work can be very convenient.)

- cope – to deal with a difficult situation (The city found it hard to cope with the giant snowstorm.)

- cordial – friendly, warm, amiable (I hate starting at a new school, but I will be cordial, and try to make new friends.)

- cultivate – prepare, work, farm (Farmers carefully cultivate their fields and crops.)

- cumulative – growing, progressive, accruing, building up (The cumulative effect of deliberately annoying your parents all day can lead to being grounded.)

- declare – state, proclaim, maintain, affirm (The governor declared a state of emergency when unexpectedly heavy rains overwhelmed the town.)

- deluge – flood, downpour, barrage (A deluge of water swept through the city after the dam burst.)

- dense – thick, heavy, having great mass (Walking through a dense forest can be difficult.)

- deplete – to use up resources or supplies (When we depleted all our supplies, we were unable to finish our science project.)

- deposit – to put into a bank to gain interest, sublimate, layer (Gradual mineral deposits lead to beautiful quartz formations in some desert areas.)

- designate – to assign someone or something (The coach designated Alan as the hockey team captain based on his excellent track record of success.)

- desperate – distressed, hopeless, last resort (When I accidentally deleted my essay just hours before it was due, I was utterly desperate to find someone to help me retrieve it.)

- deteriorate – to fall apart, decay or crumble (Friendships can deteriorate if misunderstandings aren't swiftly addressed.)

- dialogue – conversation, chat, communication (Dialogue can make or break a movie or book.)

- diligent – hardworking, particular, industrious (The diligent bus driver never missed a single day of work.)

- diminish – to make small and unimportant; to lower in value (Never diminish the importance of good health.)

- discretion – to handle quietly, with respect and out of the public eye (It's polite to handle friendship problems with discretion, rather than telling everyone about them.)

- dissent – to disagree (I dissented strongly when Gavin suggested that we should eat salad instead of burgers for lunch; I was hungry for more than lettuce!)

- dissolve – to fall apart, disintegrate or melt away into nothing (Sugar dissolves completely in hot water if you just stir it for a moment.)

- distinct – clear, clear-cut, definite (Typed letters are more distinct and easy to read than handwritten ones.)

- diversity - a wide array of things that all possess different qualities and appearances (A diversity of opinions can lead to interesting conversations.)

- domestic – homegrown, tame, kept by humans, trained (Long ago, wolves were domesticated and evolved into today's modern dogs.)

- dominate – command, control, dominate (It's impolite to dominate a conversation and not let anyone else have a turn speaking.)

- drastic – extreme, serious (In times of crises, sometimes the president must take drastic actions to protect the country.)

- duration –a length of time from the beginning to the end of an event (The duration of a year is 365 days.)

- dwell – reside or brood (I try not to dwell on the bad, but instead to stay focused on the good.)

- eclipse – blocking, covering, obscuring, blotting out (The clouds completely eclipsed the moon for a few minutes.)

- economy – wealth, financial resources, providence (The stock market is one measure of how the economy is doing.)

- eerie – creepy, haunting, to cause a sense of unease and fear (The school halls look eerie and ominous as we head to the gym for the costume party.)

- effect – result, consequence, outcome (One effect of kindness is that other people may also be kind in return.)

- efficient – to get things done in an orderly and effective manner (The most efficient way to do dishes is to work in order of dish type.)

- elaborate – to explain in detail (The doctor carefully elaborated on the instructions he gave Adam, to make sure he knew what exercises to do with his hurt leg.)

- eligible – entitled, permitted, suitable (Individuals on the honor roll are eligible for awards.)

- elude – evade, dodge, flee, avoid (The criminal continued to elude the police for many days before finally being captured.)

- encounter – run into, meet, come into contact with (It's normal to encounter challenges in the course of day-to-day life.)

- equivalent – equal to, parallel, similar, identical (When cooking, you may across recipe equivalents.)

- erupt – flare up, burst, eject (When a volcano erupts, it can often be seen from hundreds of miles away.)

- esteem – respect, admire, hold in high regard (Rosa Parks is someone held in high esteem by many people.)

- evolve – develop, change, advance (In the study of biology, one learns how animals evolve over the centuries.)

- exaggerate – overemphasize, overvalue, make something out to be larger than it actually is (The fisherman exaggerated his catch by saying it was twice as big as the fish actually was in reality.)

- excel – do extremely well (It requires discipline to excel in life.)

- exclude – to bar, keep out, ban (The "keep out" sign on the door made it clear we had been excluded from the meeting.)

- expanse – wide-open space (Standing on the mountaintop, we stared out at the vast expanse of rolling fields beneath us.)

- exploit – utilize, take advantage of, abuse (It's unkind to exploit other people's good intentions to fulfill your personal goals.)

- extinct – vanished, died off, no longer exist (Dinosaurs went extinct millions of years ago.)

- extract – take out, withdraw, remove (Reaching under the bed, the teenager extracted his backpack.)

- factor – element, part of, component (One factor of success if hard work.)

- former – past, previously, before (The former manager of the company kept in touch and offered his employees advice as they learned to deal with their new boss.)

- formulates – prepare, plan for, put together, or work out (The government formulates strategies for making people's lives easier.)

- fuse – blend, merge, bring together (The best movies fuse together things like history and science fiction to create something exciting and new.)

- futile – useless, pointless, ineffectual (Blaming people is usually a fairly futile waste of time.)

- generate – produce, cause, bring about (Solar power generates different types of energy.)

- genre – category, classification, group (Mystery is one genre in literature.)

- habitat – natural environment (A bird's natural habitat usually includes trees.)

- hazardous – dangerous, can cause harm, unsafe (Many chemicals can be hazardous to people's health.)

- hoax – joke, prank or ruse (April Fool's Day is a common day for elaborate hoaxes.)

- hostile – aggressive, belligerent, averse (Hostile words can lead to arguments and enemies.)

- idiom – expression, style of speaking (Different parts of the world use different idioms.)

- ignite – catch fire, erupt, provoke (Some people's tempers ignite faster than other's.)

- immense – vast, cosmic, enormous (The Grand Canyon is so immense that it's difficult to take it all in.)

- improvise – concoct, wing it (Comedians improve situations to provoke laughter.)

- inept – incompetent, unskilled (When it comes to anything involving hand-eye coordination, Marcus feels inept.)

- inevitable – unavoidable, bound to happen (It's inevitable that, if you're lazy and avoid your homework, you'll eventually run out of time and end up not finishing it.)

- influence – impact, control, bend to your own will (Our peers frequently have a great deal of influence on us.)

- ingenious – inventive, imaginative (The internet was once just an ingenious idea that eventually revolutionized the world.)

- innovation – original, new, novel (Every single year there are new technological innovations.)

- intimidate – frighten (New experiences can sometimes be a little intimidating.)

- jovial – good-humored, happy, cheerful (Annie is a jovial, kind person who never fails to put a smile on people's faces.

- knack – gift, talent, flair (Penny has a knack for juggling.)

- leeway – elbow room, freedom (Some teachers allow more leeway than others in judging assignments.)

- legislation – laws considered collectively, lawmaking (Congress is responsible for much of the legislation that occurs in the United States.)

- leisure – relaxation, rest, downtime (Some kids use leisure time to play video games or sports.)

- liberate – set free, release (We liberated the tiger from his cage and he raced out into the jungle.)

- likeness – resemblance, similarities (Children often have a likeness to their parents and grandparents.)

- linger – to hang around, dawdle (The sign said, "Do not linger in the halls.")

- literal – factual, word for word (A literal answer is an exact, word-for-word explanation.)

- loathe – hate, detest (Some students absolutely loathe doing homework.)

- lure – coax, tempt, persuade (The fisherman used a worm as a lure for a fish.)

- majority – large part or major group (The majority of people want to feel understood and accepted.)

- makeshift – temporary (After a hurricane, people often must live in makeshift conditions.)

- manipulate – control, exploit (It's hard to trust someone who tries to manipulate you to get what he/she wants.)

- marvel – to be amazed or astonished (Joe stood there and marveled at the incredible sunrise.)

- massive – huge, enormous (The destruction after an earthquake is often massive.)

- maximum – most, greatest (Maximum joy comes from success after self-discipline.)

- meager – limited, inadequate (One piece of bread with butter is a very meager lunch.)

- mere – bare, only, basic (That magazine cost a mere dollar.)

- migration – relocate, resettle (We watched a movie about great elephant migrations across the Sahara Desert.)

- mimic – to imitate or copy (The parrot likes to mimic my dad's singing.)

- monotonous – tedious, boring, dull (Often, parts of the learning process are monotonous but necessary.)

- negotiate – work out, discuss terms (The lawyer helped his client negotiate the very best business deal possible.)

- objective – goal, purpose or mission (Your objective in reading this study guide are to help prepare you for an exam.)

- obstacle – to get in the way of, something that needs to be overcome, blocking the way (It takes courage and perseverance to over obstacles on the path of life.)

- omniscient – all-knowing, all-wise (Sometimes it can seem like computers are omniscient, because they seem to know so much.)

- onset – at the beginning (At the onset of the disease, the person's skin first got very warm and flushed.)

- optimist – a person who looks on the bright side (An optimist is usually cheerful and confident about the future.)

- originate – where someone or something came from (The Air Force is looking into where the UFO may have originated.)

- painstaking – careful, meticulous, attentive (Engineers must do painstaking word because any lack of precision can cause a machine to malfunction.)

- paraphrase – to sum things up in a short, clear way (When reading a passage, the best way to test your understanding is to paraphrase it.)

- parody – mockery, satire (Much of literature involves a kind of parody.)

- persecute – mistreat, oppress (Bullies persecute people and make their lives miserable.)

- plummet – to drop or fall quickly (Meteors plummet to the earth at incredible speeds.)

- possess – to own (If you possess a lot of toys, you probably have to regularly clean your room.)

- poverty – lacking in wealth (Many people who grow up in poverty are far more appreciative of simple things like food and shelter.)

- precise – exact, on point (Archery requires a person to aim an arrow with extremely precise accuracy.)

- predicament – difficult situation, mess (Getting stuck in a pool of quicksand is a real predicament.)

- predict – to make an educated guess based on the facts (Weather forecasters predict upcoming storms as well as weather on a daily basis.)

- prejudice – bias, intolerance (The school declared that it would tolerate any kind of racial prejudice.)

- preliminary – opening, introductory (A preliminary introduction to a brand-new class helps tell you what you will be learning throughout the whole course.)

- primitive – ancient, antique, unsophisticated (The primitive net is probably not particularly useful for hunting.)

- priority – to put something first, such as a loved one or a particular task (Parents have the priority of always taking care of their kids first.)

- prominent – an object in clear view, an important person (The celebrity Mabel admires is a very prominent personality who appears on many TV shows.)

- propel – to move forward (Kicking your legs while in the pool will help propel you forward.)

- prosecute – take legal action, take to court (If you commit a crime, you will likely end up in court being prosecuted.)

- prosper – do well, thrive (You have to work hard if you intend to prosper in life.)

- provoke – to irritate, stir up trouble (Provoking bees is a very bad idea which is likely to get you stung.)

- pursue – go after (The detective pursued the criminal all the way down the block.)

- quest – journey, trip, mission to seek something out (In literature, protagonists often undertake great quests which takes them thousands of miles away from home.)

- recount – describe, relate, tell (Eagerly, Jessica recounted the story of how she pitched a no-hitter.)

- refuge – shelter, sanctuary (The wildlife refuge is a beautiful place, full of rescued pandas.)

- reinforce – to shore up, lend additional support (Before the hurricane, the town reinforced the dam with many sandbags.)

- reluctant – unwilling or uncooperative (The horse was extremely reluctant to leave its stall on a cold, snowy day.)

- remorse – great sadness (After making a big mistake, a person may feel a great deal of remorse.)

- remote – located far away (The cabin was on a remote mountaintop, 100 miles from the city.)

- resolute – purposeful (Being resolute means accepting difficulties and remaining determined to reach a goal.)

- restrain – to prevent from leaving, to hold on to (A seat belt is a common type of restraint used to protect people in case of a car accident.)

- retaliate – fight back (If somehow hurts your feelings, sometimes your instinct may be to retaliate, but that isn't always helpful.)

- retrieve – to go and get (Often, people train their dogs to retrieve a ball or other objects.)

- rigorous – meticulous, careful, diligent (A rigorous study of any subject is necessary if you really plan to get something out of a class you take.)

- rural – countryside, rustic (The opposite of a city like Manhattan is a rural place like a mountain town.)

- salvage – rescue, save, recover (After a flood or fire, people have to try to salvage all they can.)

- sanctuary – a haven or safe place (It's nice to feel like your home is a sanctuary at the end of a long day.)

- siege – military operation (The Romans were famous for their wartime sieges.)

- significant – of importance, having great value (Family and friends are significant parts of most people's lives.)

- solar – relating to the sun (Solar power is becoming more and more common in the world, especially in places with desert climates.)

- soothe – pacify, settle, subdue (The new mother walked the baby back and forth to soothe it.)

- stationary – to not move, be immobile or stay in one place (A car in a parking lot is stationary.)

- stifle – impede, suffocate, smother (The heat at noon can feel stifling in some parts of the country.)

- strive – aspire, attempt, try (It's a noble goal to strive consistently to help others.)

- subordinate – submissive, deferring to those above you (Unless you own your own company, you'll likely be working as someone else's subordinate.)

- subsequent – next (After grabbing an umbrella, Brad's subsequent action was to walk out into the rain.)

- superior – above others (Grocery store brands like to claim they are each superior to their competitors' products.)

- supplement – to add to (Vitamins can be used as supplements to regular healthy eating.)

- swarm – come together in a group (The swarm of kids rushed out of the school building.)

- tangible – something that can be physically touched (A hug is a tangible symbol of love between a parent and a child.)

- terminate – to end, cancel or do away with (The computer will terminate a program if certain errors occur.)

- terrain – the surroundings or land in a given area (The rough terrain we are hiking on will take us several hours to cross.)

- trait – attribute or quality (Honesty is generally considered an excellent personality trait.)

- transform – to change shape (Some toys have buttons that you push in order to transform their shapes.)

- transport – to move, carry or travel (Transporting heavy objects can be exhausting.)

- treacherous – disloyal, unsafe, duplicitous (Rough waters can be treacherous to swim in.)

- unanimous – everyone in agreement on a specific topic, idea or decision (The committee unanimously voted to postpone the event until more people had committed to helping.)

- unique – special, unlike any other (The Hope Diamond is utterly unique due to its size and color.

- unruly – rowdy, disorderly (The unruly students left the teacher exhausted by the end of the day.)

- urban – inner city (Urban areas can contain a surprising number of animals if you look closely.)

- vacate – to leave, evacuate or empty (In three days, we will vacate our motel and fly home.)

- verdict – a final ruling or decision (The jury returned a guilty verdict after hours of deliberation.)

- verge – on the edge, brink, rim or border (Standing on the verge of a cliff can make some people queasy.)

- vibrant – spirited, lively (The little girl's vibrant smile always made people cheer up around her.)

- vital – important, essential to life (Oxygen and water are two elements that are vital to life.)

- vow – a promise, giving your word, making an oath (I vow to make the most of my senior year.)

Chapter 3: Quantitative Reasoning and Mathematics Achievement

Your ISEE Lower Level Exam will contain a section on Quantitative Reasoning and another section on Mathematics Achievements. Though each section involves math in one form or another, each tests a different skill set. That said, both sections include some of the same components. Those components include:

- Multiplication
- Division
- Addition
- Subtraction
- Word problems

You may be working with:

- Even and odd numbers
- Prime numbers and prime factorization
- Percentages
- Squaring numbers
- Finding square roots
- Exponents
- Averages
- Measurements and units of measurement:
    - weight
    - length
    - volume
    - speed

The questions in each of the four study guide practice tests, as well as the ones you'll face on your official exam, will test your skills and abilities to:
- Estimate
- Problem-solve
- Interpret information
- Analyze data
- Make predictions
- Draw conclusions
- Understand concepts
- Draw logical conclusions

Quantitative Reasoning

Quantitative Reasoning is something we all use on a daily basis, such as if your mom tells you to measure out a pound of apples to make pies, but it's also something many of us don't think too much about. Similar to Verbal Reasoning, Quantitative Reasoning is more about the skills you have and how you apply them, as opposed to the information you have learned in a classroom.

Quantitative Reasoning tests your abilities to problem-solve, using mathematical thinking to reach a conclusion. It comes down to clear and critical thinking, your skills in regards to how you think mathematically and how you use those skills and abilities in everyday life.

This study guide will help you to exercise these skills and prepare yourself for your ISEE Lower Level Exam.

To complete the test in a timely manner:

- Read the directions carefully.
- Then carefully read each question. Each question will be asking you to find something specific.
- Review each of the possible multiple-choice answers.
- Eliminate the answers you know don't fit the question first.
- Then move on to the answers you feel are possibilities.
- Think about the information you've been given to logically decide what answer is the best solution for each question.

Some of the key things you will want to think about while you are reading the questions and considering the answer options are:

- What are you being asked to figure out?
- What information is important and what information doesn't matter to finding the answer?
- Separate out any text or information that you decide is not important.
- Are there answers that don't fit? If so, remove them as options and focus on the ones that are possible.
- Is this something you need an exact answer for or do you just need to make a guess?

Mathematical Achievement

The Mathematical Achievements section is designed to test the math skills you have learned over the course of your entire academic career. The ISEE Lower Level Exam will test what you know and what you have retained up until this point.

The questions on the official exam will include arithmetic equations, geometry and word problems. In this study guide, you will have the opportunity to exercise those skills in the four separate practice tests.

Since you are not allowed to use a calculator while completing the official ISEE Lower Level Exam, you should not use one on any of the practice tests in your study guide. The official exam allows you to use the blank spaces in your exam booklet as scratch paper, so you can use scratch paper while completing the practice tests.

You may find that there are questions on the ISEE Lower Level Exam that you don't know and haven't seen before. This is because you may not have been taught that content yet. Use the skills and knowledge that you do have to work the problem out and choose the most logical answer.

Some answers will come easier than others. Remember to use your time wisely. If you come to a question you just can't figure out, skip it and come back if you have time in the end. Otherwise, you may find yourself in a position where you've spent all your time trying to solve one problem and don't get a chance to do any of the others before time runs out.

Key Study Points for Quantitative Reasoning and Mathematics

These are some of the basic mathematical operations, symbols and expressions you may need on the exam:

Arithmetic

One of the most important things to remember when you are working out a math equation is the order in which you're supposed to figure it out. To that end, the Order of Operations is listed below.

Step 1. Solve any equations in parentheses first. i.e., $4 + 8 (6 \times 6 - 4) + 16 = ?$ The first step you would take to solve this equation would be to solve $(6 \times 6 - 4)$.

Step 2. Simplify exponents. Combine the numbers you have and their exponents that are also the same. i.e., $9 \times 12^3 + 12^3 + 12^3 + 54 = ?$ To solve this, first combine the exponents. $12^3 + 12^3 + 12^3 = 36^9$.

Step 3. Multiply, then divide. i.e., $5 + 4 \times 12 - 3 = ?$ Solve 4×12 first. $4 \times 12 = 48$, so the equation then becomes $5 + 39 - 4$.

Step 4. Do any addition and subtraction. i.e., $5 + 39 = 44 - 4 = 40$

Division

While taking the ISEE exam you will be pressed for time. With that in mind, there are a few quick tricks that may help you to quickly determine if one number is divisible by another. Those quick tricks include:

- If a number ends in an even number then it is always divisible by 2.
- If you can add the digits of a larger number together, you can determine if the number is divisible by 3 or 9 if the sum of the digits is divisible by 3 or 9. i.e., 123 → 1 + 2 + 3 = 6. The 6 can be divided by 3, so the number 123 is divisible by 3.
- A number is divisible by 4 if the last two digits of the number are divisible by 4. i.e., 256 → 56÷4 =14. 56 is divisible by 4, so 256 is divisible by 4.
- If a number ends in zero or 5, the number is always divisible by 5.
- If a number ends in zero, it's always divisible by 10.

Working with Even and Odd Numbers	
Addition	**Multiplication**
Even Number + Even Number = Even Answer	Even Number × Even Number = Even Answer
Odd Number + Odd Number = Even Answer	Even Number × Odd Number = Even Answer
Odd Number + Even Number = Odd Answer	Odd Number × Even Number = Odd Answer

Standard Units of Measurement
Measuring Length in Standard Units:
<ul><li>1 foot (ft) = 12 inches (in)</li><li>1 yard (yd) = 3 feet (ft)</li><li>1 mile (mi) = 1,760 yards (yd)</li><li>1 acre (ac) = 43,560 square feet (sq ft)</li></ul>
Measuring Volume in Standard Units:
<ul><li>1 cup (c) = 8 fluid ounces (fl oz)</li><li>1 pint (pt) = 2 cups (c)</li><li>1 quart (qt) = 2 pints (pt)</li><li>1 gallon (gal) = 4 quarts (qt)</li></ul>
Measuring Weight in Standard Units:
<ul><li>1 pound (lb or lbs) = 16 ounces (oz)</li><li>1 ton (tn) = 2,000 pounds (lb or lbs)</li></ul>
Measuring Speed in Standard Units:
<ul><li>1 mile per hour (mph) = 1.4666 feet per second (ft sec)</li></ul>

Metric Units of Measurement

Measuring Length in Metric Units:
- 1 centimeter (cm) = 10 millimeters (mm)
- 1 meter (m) = 100 centimeters (cm)
- 1 kilometer (km) = 1,000 meters (m)

Measuring Volume in Metric Units:
- 1 liter (l) = 1,000 milliliters (ml)
- 1 liter (l) = 1,000 cubic centimeters (cm^3)

Measuring Weight in Metric Units:
- 1 gram (g) = 1,000 milligrams (mg)
- 1 kilogram (kg) = 1,000 grams (g)

Measuring Speed in Metric Units:
- 1 kilometer per hour (km hr) = 0.277778 meters per second (m sec)

Mathematic Terms

GCF: Greatest common factor: The greatest positive number that a number or set of numbers can be divided by evenly.

LCM = Least common multiple: The lowest number that a number or set of numbers can be divided by evenly.

LCD = Least common denominator: The lowest denominator between a set of fractions.

Standard and Expanded Form: Using the number 111 as the example ...
Expanded Form = 100 + 10 + 1
Standard Form = 111

Multiplication: In a word problem, the word "of" means that you are multiplying and the word "is" refers to the sum. i.e., the sum of 12 and 2 is 24.

Unending numbers in decimals: When there is a number or numbers after the decimal point it means that the number continues to repeat. i.e., in the number $167.\overline{333}$, the threes repeat infinitely.

Mean: The average of a set of numbers.

Median: The median is the middle number in a set of numbers. For example, if you have the set of numbers 1, 2, 3, 4, 5, 6, 7, 8, 9, then the median number would be 5. The key to finding the median is to first arrange the data in order from least to greatest.

Mode: The mode is the number that is most common in a number set. For example, if you have the set of numbers 1, 2, 3, 1, 3, 4, 1, 5, the number 1 appears twice, and the number 3 appears three times, so the mode would be 3 since it occurs more than any of the other numbers.

Mathematics Symbols

< Less Than ≤ Less Than or Equal to	> Greater Than ≥ Greater Than or Equal to
π Pi **OR** 3.14159	= Equal to ≠ Not Equal
√ Square Root	$\|x\|$ Absolute Value

Numeric Place Values

Whole Numbers, Positive Numbers & Values to the Left of the Decimal Point	Negative Numbers and Place Values to the Right of the Decimal Point

Equations for Finding Area

Triangle	Area= ½ × base ×width	A=1/2 × b × w
Rectangle	Area = width × height	A=w × h
Square	Area = $height^2$	A=h^2
Circle	Area = $\pi \times radius^2$	$A = \pi r^2$
Trapezoid	Area = ½ × (top width + base width) × height	A= ½ (t + b) h

Prime Numbers and Factorization

Prime numbers are whole numbers or integers that are greater than 1 and their only factors are the number 1 and the number itself. The number 2 is the lowest prime number, and the numbers zero and 1 are never prime.

There are many prime numbers. These include: 2, 3, 5, 7, 11, 17, 19, 23 and 29.

Prime factorization consists of finding a given prime factor and putting it into a specific expression. For example, when expressed by prime factorization the number 24 can be displayed as $2^3 \times 3$ or as $2 \times 2 \times 2 \times 3$.

Percentages, Decimals and Fractions

Percentages, decimals and fractions are all portions of a whole number. They can also all be converted to one another. The table below illustrates this:

Sample Chart of Fractions, Decimals and Percentages Representing the Same Values		
Fractions	**Percentages**	**Decimals**
1/10	10%	0.10
2/10 = 1/5	20%	0.2
1/4	25%	0.25
3/10	30%	0.3
1/3	33.3%	0.3
4/10 = 2/5	40%	0.4
5/10 = 1/2	50%	0.5
6/10 = 3/5	60%	0.6
2/3	66.6%	0.6
7/10	70%	0.7
3/4	75%	0.75
8/10 = 4/5	80%	0.8
9/10	90%	0.9
10/10 = 1	100%	1.0

Remember that the top number in a fraction is always the numerator and the bottom number is the denominator. In the event that you come across a fraction like $4\frac{1}{8}$, this is a mixed number. The number in the same place as the 4 in the example is a whole number.

Roots and Square Roots

To square a number means to multiply the number by itself. i.e., $2 \times 2 = 2^2$. When you square a number, the result is known as a **perfect square**.

In mathematics, there are three types of roots:

- The root of a number
- Square root – i.e., $n^2 = n \times n$
- Cube root – i.e., $n^3 = n \times n \times n$

Some key points to remember about roots:

- You cannot have a perfect square under a square root.
- Denominators do not have radical numbers.
- Fractions cannot be in a square root.

Exponents

Exponents tell you how many times a number is multiplied by itself. They're also a way to put an equation into simpler terms.

Some examples of exponents are:

- $n \times n \times n \times b \times b \times c \times c \times c \times c \times c \times c = n^3 \times b^2 \times c^6$
- $16^8 = 16 \times 16 \times 16 \times 16 \times 16 \times 16 \times 16 \times 16$

Averages

Averages have three parts:

1. The number of numbers involved
2. The total of the numbers involved
3. The average.

The average is also called the mean. The average is the total of all the numbers involved divided to find the middle number between all those in the set. For example:

Step 1. You are given the set of numbers 2, 4, 6, 8, 10, 12, 14, 16, 18, 20.
Step 2. To find the average, add the numbers.
2 + 4 + 6 + 8 + 10 + 12 +14 + 16 + 18 + 20 = 110.
Step 3. Divide the number of numbers in the set by the total.
In this case, there are 10 numbers in this set. 110 ÷ 10 = 11
Step 4. Therefore, the average of this number set is 11.

Chapter 4: Reading Comprehension

The Reading Comprehension section of the ISEE Lower Level Exam focuses on how you understand and retain the information you read.

Some of the Reading Comprehension skills you will use in this study guide as well as during your official exam will include:

- Summarizing the text that you've been given.
  - Reading a passage or a piece of information. Briefly mentally summarize the information you have read and sum up what you think it means or, in some cases, what you think the writer is trying to say.
- Making sensible and logical inferences.
  - Reading a passage or piece of information and deciding what the writer is saying. This usually isn't something that the writer is clearly stating. Rather, the writer will hint and provide subtle clues to the stance he or she is taking.
- Comparing and contrasting.
  - Reading a passage and being able to pick out the things that are similar or different.
- Sequencing things.
  - Your ability to sort through the written information you have been given and put it in order from beginning to end, most relevant to least. For sequencing, you will want to look for key words such as first, next, then, finally, before, beginning with, etc.
- Drawing conclusions based on the text and how you have interpreted it.
  - Reading the information in the text and deciding what the end result was, based on the information you were given by the writer, as well as the information that you feel the writer was implying.

To develop your reading comprehension skills, always consider:
- The main idea of the text you are reading.
- Any information that supports the main point or idea.
- The overall tone or mood of the passage or text you are reading.
- How a text is organized.
- The wording used in a text.

The Reading Comprehension test is made up of five separate passages. Those passages will each have five questions.

Much like the official exam, this study guide includes four practice exams. In each of the four practice exams, similar to your official exam, you will find a Reading

Comprehension section. Each Reading Comprehension section has five separate passages. Each passage is followed by five multiple-choice questions. The passages will have topics that relate to literature, history, science and modern life. The questions for each passage will be about:

- The text that was written.
- The meaning or main idea.
- How the text made you feel or the things it made you think about.
- The picture it painted for you.
- What inferences you are able to reasonably draw based on the information you have been given.

It is important that on the official ISEE Lower Level exam, as well as the practice tests in this study guide, you carefully read each passage. Take the time to read through each passage a second time to ensure you have not missed anything.

Once you have read the passage, carefully read each question. Be sure that you understand what each question is asking and then review each of the multiple-choice answers. Eliminate any of the options that do not make sense or which are unrelated to the text. If there is more than one answer that you think could be right, take the time to review the question again.

Remember that you can always reread the passage to find the answer if you need to. It can also be helpful to ask yourself these questions as you read the passage:
- What is the passage about?
- What points is the passage making clear?
- What visual images does this passage create?
- What does the mood of the passage make me feel?

These key questions can help you to narrow down your answer choices.

Pay attention to details as you're reading so that you don't miss key information such as a particularly important word.

In your practice tests, you will find questions that have very direct answers. You will also have questions that will require you to draw logical conclusions based on the information implied in the passage.

Reading comprehension isn't simply about being able to pick out the exact items that are clearly in front of you. It's about the vocabulary being used, and your ability to comprehend it. There will be times when a word itself may not make sense, but the passage as a whole or the picture the words create will give you the answer.

In your practice tests, you will find poems that paint a picture. The questions will require you to pull apart what you are reading. A sentence may not make sense on its own. For example, if you read a poem that says "the tides will turn," you may think about water and changing direction. However, when you read the passage as a whole it may read, "Your betrayal is felt, the tides will turn, and I will have my revenge." The passage as a whole means that someone betrayed another person, things will change for the people involved and the person who was wronged will get the chance to hurt the person who hurt them first.

You use reading comprehension all the time, across all different school subjects. This means you are constantly exercising your reading comprehension skills, expanding your vocabulary and understanding more and more about the written word.

Key Study Points for Reading Comprehension

The Reading Comprehension practice tests and the official exam both contain passages for you to read. All the information you need will be either directly in the passage, implied or you will be asked about an opinion.

The passages you will be given on the ISEE Exam will mostly be pulled from other texts. Articles may come from things like classic or contemporary books, various articles and an array of journals.

The test will be timed. Time yourself and practice often. The more you practice, the better and faster you will become. Read anything—a library book, your school textbook, magazines; it doesn't matter. Make a point to pick out the main idea and the key facts. This will help you to hone your reading and understanding skills, read and retain information faster and help you to perform at your best.

Skim Reading or Reading Verbatim

There are different ways to approach reading comprehension questions. You may choose to skim read first and go back for more details later or you may choose to read verbatim from the start. Skim reading involves quickly reading through a piece of literature to get the general idea of what the text is about. Reading verbatim, on the other hand, is reading every single word.

These two reading styles are vastly different and neither style is a one-size-fits-all. Sometimes it's better to skim the passage to get a general idea, review the questions, then go back and pick out the key points you need to answer them. Other times, it's better to read the whole passage at length, then go over the questions and answer them, only going back to the passage if absolutely necessary.

While you're studying for the exam it's important that you practice your approach. Find out how you best retain information and how fast you read. Time yourself when you're practicing to ensure that you can get through five brief passages in the time the official exam allows.

Be sure that as you answer the questions you check the passage to ensure they're right; sometimes our memories fail us, so it never hurts to double-check.

Mentally Summarizing

After you have read over the passage take a moment to think about what you've read and mentally summarize it.

- Consider the details that are important and the information that is just fluff.
- Tentatively arrange the details, timelines and important information into a brief outline for yourself.
- Focus on important details that pop out.

The Beginning and the End

Pay attention to the opening and closing lines of passages. It's not uncommon for the author to leave key details in these places. Often the opening lines will contain the main idea and the closing lines will summarize the main idea.

Attention to Detail

It's important that as you read the passages and the questions, you pay attention to detail. As you read, ask yourself questions such as:
- What is the passage about?
- What is the main point?
  Are there dates, times, people or places that jump out as being important?
-
Consider the emotions, mood and tone of the passage:
- Are there descriptive emotions?
- Is the tone positive or negative?
- Does the author seem to express a strong opinion in the passage?

Make Inferences

Some questions will ask you to make an inference, to choose an answer based on logic and reason. This requires you to use your own personal judgment. When making an inference:

- Find and understand the main idea.
- Logically consider what the author thinks next.
- Look for things that can be concluded but are not said outright.

General Ideas

You may get a feeling based on something that's written. For instance, if you read a passage that says, "Annabel was cold and wet as she ran through her front door after work," the sentence doesn't say it was raining on her way home, but you can logically conclude that it was raining when she left work and that she was soaked when she got home.

Put yourself in the writer's shoes. Think about how the writer says he/she feels about the topic in question.

Consider the context of what the writer is saying. What does the writer say in order to develop the topic? What supportive words, phrases or emotions are used?

Ultimately, practice reading at different paces, see how well you comprehend and retain information at different paces and decide what the best pace and approach is for you. Focus on key points and don't worry if you have to take a moment to reread a passage to confirm an answer.

Chapter 5: Essay Writing

For your official ISEE Lower Level Exam, you will have 30 minutes to carefully read over your topic, make notes and organize your thoughts, and write a detailed essay related to the essay topic you have been given. Writing an essay is an effective way to allow you to demonstrate your organization, writing and creative skills.

Topics for the official exam are randomly selected to ensure that the same topics are not on the test every time. The ISEE exam chooses topics that are geared towards the grade level and children who are expected to take the exam. This is done in anticipation of gaining your attention and getting your mental wheels turning, to ensure you are interested, if not inspired to write about the assigned topic.

When you take your official exam the answer booklet will provide you with a section to write notes, organize thoughts or create an outline. You will also be given two full pages to write your essay. This portion of the exam will be written in blue or black ink as opposed to the #2 pencil that you used in the other four parts of the exam. You can write the essay in print or cursive, whichever your preference.

In anticipation of your exam requirements, each essay topic in the four study guide practice tests will also provide you with a section for notes, and for writing your essay.

Read the essay topic carefully. Take a few moments to think about the topic and what you would like to write regarding it. Organize your thoughts using the method that is most effective for you.

Then take those thoughts and put them into a well-organized and detailed essay. Write clearly, with complete thoughts, and as much detail as you can. Remember that you are only given a half-hour to complete this portion of the exam so be sure to use your time wisely to ensure you have the time to complete your essay.

Key Study Points for Essay Writing

The essay portion of the ISEE Lower Level Exam is the only section of the exam that is not multiple choice and it is also not graded by the testing center. However, it is very important to your admissions application, and the schools you are applying to will be reading your essay. So it's very important that you write a well-thought-out essay.

So, how do you write a good essay?

Below you will find a list of strategies that will help:

- Read your essay topic carefully.

- Once you have read your essay topic over and know what you need to write about, it's time to make a plan.
  - Take a few moments to plan.
  - Make notes on the things you want to write.
  - Note a few reasons that you feel a specific way about the topic.
  - Decide on what supporting information you want to include.
  - Organize your thoughts and decide the order in which you would like to write things.

Once you have a good idea of what you want to write and the order in which you want to put your thoughts, it is important that you stick to your plan.

You shouldn't spend too much time on brainstorming or putting together an outline. Leave yourself plenty of time to write.

While writing, be sure to:

- Follow your plan.
- Remember the key points you wanted to make.
- Make your opinion or position clear.
- Give clear reasoning and support.
- Write in detail.
- Make sure you use wording that is clear and descriptive.
- Consider who will be reading this.
- Offer good reasons for why you feel the way you do about the topic you are writing about.
- Take the time to check your outline along the way.
- Ensure you stay on track and make all of your points.
- Maintain a good flow and don't let yourself wander off topic.
- Come back around to your key point, summing up the conclusion where you started at the beginning.
- Use correct grammar, spelling, punctuation, etc.

Test 1: Verbal Reasoning

In the Verbal Reasoning section of this practice test, you will find practice questions that require you to do one of two things. You will either choose the **synonym** that means the same or similar thing to the **CAPITALIZED** word beside each numbered question, or you will be asked to choose from the multiple-choice answers to select the word or phrase that most logically **completes the sentence** you're given.

Synonym Directions: For the following practice test questions, read the **CAPITALIZED** word carefully. Choose the multiple-choice answer that means the same or close to the same as the **CAPITALIZED** word.

(1)   ABOLISH

(A)   start

(B)   instigate

(C)   riot

(D)   eliminate

(2)   BARREN

(A)   fruitful

(B)   bland

(C)   desolate

(D)   invigorating

(3)   CAUTIOUSLY

(A)   calculating

(B)   vigilantly

(C)   hopelessly

(D)   brawny

(4)   DENSE

(A)   accelerate

(B)   opaque

(C)   listless

(D)   transparent

(5)   EVADE

(A)   surrender

(B)   elude

(C)   transgression

(D)   porous

(6)   FUTILE

(A)   pointless

(B)   sharpen

(C)   pointedly

(D)   aspire

(7)   GIGANTIC

(A)   minuscule

(B)   trifling

(C)   omniscient

(D)   colossal

(8)   HOAX

(A)   strategy

(B)   illusion

(C)   swindle

(D)   indomitable

(9)   IDENTICAL

(A)   similar

(B)   minded

(C)   duplicate

(D)   different

(10)   JOVIAL

(A)   cheerful

(B)   begrudging

(C)   miserable

(D)   resplendent

(11)   KIN

(A)   acquaintance

(B)   coworker

(C)   people

(D)   relations

(12)   LITERAL

(A)   tomfoolery

(B)   fictional

(C)   accurate

(D)   figurative

(13)   MONARCH

(A)   sovereign

(B)   mother

(C)   subordinate

(D)   peasant

(14)   NEGOTIATE

(A)   disagreement

(B)   collaborate

(C)   impassive

(D)   superfluous

(15)   OVERTHROW

(A)   surrender

(B)   bolster

(C)   support

(D)   topple

(16)   PAINSTAKING

(A)   reckless

(B)   meticulous

(C)   freewheeling

(D)   careless

(17)   QUEST

(A)   expedition

(B)   research

(C)   chastise

(D)   unyielding

Sentence Completion Directions: For the following practice test questions, choose the answer that logically completes each sentence. Then read the question to yourself again with the answer you've chosen to ensure that it still makes sense to you, before moving on to the next one.

Test 1 Sentence Completion

(1)   The weather report said we are expecting snow and that four to six inches will ____.

(A)   precipitate

(B)   accumulate

(C)   assimilate

(D)   enunciate

(2)   I walk ____ through the park because it is so cold.

(A)   lazily

(B)   superfluously

(C)   briskly

(D)   cautiously

(3)   I used my father's tools and lumber to ____ my project for social studies.

(A)   demolish

(B)   convert

(C)   mend

(D)   construct

(4)   The customer was ____ with the broken television he received.

(A)   dissatisfied

(B)   thrilled

(C)   overwhelmed

(D)   ecstatic

(5)   No one believed Evelyn's stories because ___.

(A)   she always told the truth.

(B)   she always exaggerated the truth.

(C)   she always appraised the truth.

(D)   she always ascertained the truth.

(6)   I needed a winter coat, gloves and boots because ____.

(A)   it was balmy outside.

(B)   it was sweltering outside.

(C)   it was frigid outside.

(D)   it was brisk outside.

(7)   I was ____ excited to go to the carnival with my family.

(A)   sarcastically

(B)   overwhelmingly

(C)   controversially

(D)   genuinely

(8)   The knight was absolutely ____ when he charged the dragon with his sword drawn to save the damsel.

(A)   heroic

(B)   cowardly

(C)   fearful

(D)   cumbersome

(9)   The cut was deep, so the doctor had to ____ the wound before closing it.

(A)   bandage

(B)   irrigate

(C)   stitch

(D)   cover

(10)   The horizon runs ____ along the bay.

(A)   vertically

(B)   perpendicular

(C)   horizontally

(D)   centered

(11)   In my ____ time, I enjoy reading, painting and dancing.

(A)   preoccupied

(B)   diverted

(C)   employed

(D)   leisure

(12)   It went against my ____ judgment to steal the rival school's mascot.

(A)   moral

(B)   depraved

(C)   nefarious

(D)   shameless

(13)   The Greek gods are some of the most ____.

(A)   well-known people in history.

(B)   well-known myths of all time.

(C)   well-known figures in Roman times.

(D)   well-placed statues in history.

(14)   Connie was so engrossed in her novel that she was ____ to everything going on around her.

(A)   distracted

(B)   mismanaged

(C)   oblivious

(D)   torn

(15)   The best place in the city to see the stars is the top of Mount Olive, but you need a/an _____ telescope to take there.

(A)   moored

(B)   anchored

(C)   rooted

(D)   portable

(16)   The body shop gave me a/an _____ for the cost of repairs.

(A)   quote

(B)   receipt

(C)   invoice

(D)   charge

(17)   My little sister was so excited _____ go for ice cream that she wore herself out and fell asleep before we arrived.

(A)   to

(B)   too

(C)   two

(D)   None of the above.

Test 1: Quantitative Reasoning

Directions: In this section, you will find a variety of questions that test your quantitative reasoning skills. The questions in this section will involve a variety of mathematical skills including mathematical operations, measurements, probability, logical reasoning and more. You will be provided with additional information such as graphs or shapes if they are needed for a specific question.

Read each of the questions and answers carefully. If unsure, consider what information is provided with each possible answer. Eliminate the answers you know don't fit until you reach the most logical answer.

(1)   Annabelle is ordering bells for the Christmas parade. She knows how many reindeer are in the parade, how many bells go on each reindeer and how many bells come in a bag. How does Annabelle figure out how many bags (b) to order?

(A) b = number of reindeer + number of bells on each reindeer

(B) b = number of bells needed ÷ number of bells in each bag

(C) b = number of bells in each bag – number of reindeer

(D) b = number of reindeer × number of bells on each reindeer

(2)   Philip scored 12 points in his first game (f), 10 points in his second game (s) and 22 points in his third game (t). How would Philip figure out his average points per game?

(A) $f + s + t$ = average points per game

(B) $(f + s + t) \div 3$ = average points per game

(C) $(f \div 3) + (s \div 3) + (t \div 3)$ = average points per game

(D) $(f + s + t) \times 3$ = average points per game

(3)   Based on the chart, which order best shows Jason's fruit sales in order from most sales to least?

(A)   Oranges, Apples, Grapes, Bananas

(B)   Grapes, Bananas, Oranges, Apples

(C)   Bananas, Grapes, Apples, Oranges

(D)   Grapes, Oranges, Bananas, Apples

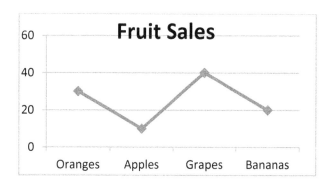

(4)   Jessica loves to have a cup of tea every morning to start her day. She is going away for a work trip for two weeks. A box of tea has five tea bags in it. If she will be gone for 14 days, how many boxes of tea is she likely to need?

(A)   Jessica will need 1 box of tea for her trip.

(B)   Jessica will need 2 boxes of tea for her trip.

(C)   Jessica will need 3 boxes of tea for her trip.

(D)   Jessica will need 4 boxes of tea for her trip.

(5)   There are five athletics teams at a school. Which team has the least number of team members?

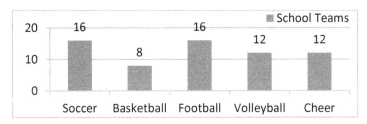

(A)   The soccer team

(B)   The basketball team

(C)   The football team

(D)   The cheer squad

(6)   There are three blank walls in an office. Wall A is 24 inches long, Wall B is 12 inches long and Wall C is 36 inches long. The painting someone bought to put up in the office is 11 inches high and 29 inches long. Which wall will the painting fit on?

(A)   Wall A

(B)   Wall B

(C)   Wall C

(D)   Any of the walls.

(7)   A desk weighs 15 lbs. What does the abbreviation lb. stand for?

(A)   Grams

(B)   Pounds

(C)   Ounces

(D)   Yards

(8)   There are a total of 24 students in the class. If 30% of the class is out sick, roughly how many students are absent?

(A)   7 students are out sick.

(B)   17 students are out sick.

(C)   16 students are out sick.

(D)   11 students are out sick.

(9)   Which equation properly expresses the sum of negative thirty-two and ninety is fifty-eight?

(A)   -32 + 90 = 58

(B)   -32 × 90 = 58

(C)   32 + 58 = 90

(D)   -32 – 90 = 58

(10)   What is the median of a set of numbers?

(A)   The middle of a set of numbers when placed in order

(B)   The average of a set of numbers

(C)   The total of a set of numbers

(D)   The most common number in a set of numbers

(11)   There are 4 black chairs, 3 green chairs, 11 red chairs, 9 yellow chairs and 16 blue chairs. What is the median number of chairs?

(A)   43

(B)   9

(C)   11

(D)   16

(12)   To find the area of a triangle, what equation will you use?

(A)   ½(base × height) = Area

(B) $radius^2\pi$ = Area

(C)   base + height = Area

(D)   base × height × depth = Area

(13)   In $\frac{2}{5}$, the number 5 is what part of the fraction?

(A)   Numerator

(B)   Mixed number

(C)   Denominator

(D)   Whole number

(14)   If you are calculating the speed of a car, what unit of measurement do you typically use?

(A)   Miles per hour

(B)   Inches per hour

(C)   Yards per hour

(D)   Feet per hour

(15)   In the equation 1 + 6 (4 + 9 − 3) (8 + 8) − 12, what do you do first?

(A)   Do the multiplication first

(B)   Do the addition first

(C)   Do the calculations in parentheses first

(D)   Do the subtraction first

(16)   If the elephant weighs 10 tons and the hippo weighs 8, the elephant's weight is __ the hippos.

(A)   the same as

(B)   less than

(C)   equal to

(D)   greater than

(17)   How do you write three hundred fifteen in expanded form?

(A)   315

(B)   300 + 10 + 5

(C)   3 + 1 + 5

(D)   Three hundred fifteen

(18)   The semitruck does 15 miles per gallon of fuel. Diesel fuel is $3.25 a gallon. What is the approximate cost of gas if the semitruck needs to drive 675 miles to its next stop?

(A)   It will cost about $145 to make the trip.

(B)   It will cost about $168 to make the trip.

(C)   It will cost about $135 to make the trip.

(D)   It will cost about $115 to make the trip.

(19)   Avery is making apple pies for the bakery. The bakery sells about 30 pies a day. If one pie requires 15 apples, approximately how many apples will Avery need to make his pies?

(A)   Approximately 250 apples.

(B)   Approximately 350 apples.

(C)   Approximately 450 apples.

(D)   Approximately 550 apples.

(20)   What is the GCF of 224, 682 and 348?

(A)   2

(B)   12

(C)   24

(D)   48

(21)   What is the LCM of 7, 14 and 56?

(A)   7

(B)   14

(C)   59

(D)   56

(22)   What are the prime factors of 489 other than 1 and 489?

(A)   2 and 3.

(B)   48 and 9.

(C)   16 and 18.

(D)   163 and 3.

(23)   Which of the following numbers is a prime number?

(A)   2

(B)   4

(C)   6

(D)   8

(24)   Which of the following numbers is a prime number?

(A)   30

(B)   33

(C)   37

(D)   39

(25)   Which of the following numbers is a multiple of 12?

(A)   107

(B)   122

(C)   144

(D)   200

(26) Which of the following numbers is a multiple of 115?

(A) 100

(B) 135

(C) 265

(D) 345

(27) What equation has the solution $\frac{11}{30}$?

(A) $\frac{1}{5} - \frac{5}{10} + \frac{10}{15}$

(B) $\frac{1}{30} + \frac{9}{30} - \frac{12}{30}$

(C) $\frac{1}{15} + \frac{3}{15} + \frac{9}{15} + \frac{12}{15}$

(D) $\frac{50}{30} - \frac{30}{30}$

(28) What is the LCD of $\frac{12}{14}, \frac{10}{25}, \frac{8}{16}$?

(A) 70

(B) 2800

(C) 1620

(D) 198

(29) Which of the following correctly shows the common factors of 8, 32 and 68?

(A) 1, 2 and 3

(B) 1, 2 and 4

(C) 1, 2 and 6

(D) 1, 2 and 8

(30)   If there is a 5 to 1 ratio of vanilla cookies to chocolate cookies, what does this mean?

(A)   For every five vanilla cookies, there is one chocolate cookie.

(B)   There are the same number of vanilla cookies as there are chocolate ones.

(C)   For every five chocolate cookies, there is one vanilla cookie.

(D)   There are 5 percent more vanilla cookies than chocolate ones.

(31)   How is the equation $|x + j|$ written as a word problem?

(A)   The absolute value of x and j.

(B)   The sum of x and j.

(C)   The value of x and j.

(D)   The root of x and j.

(32)   How is the equation $\frac{1}{4} + 12\frac{3}{8} \times 6^2$ expressed as a word problem?

(A)   One fourth increased by twelve and three-eighths multiplied by six squared.

(B)   The sum of twelve and three-eighths and six squared increased by one fourth.

(C)   Two-eighths increased by twelve and three-eighths multiplied by six to the second power.

(D)   The sum of six squared and twelve and three-eighths increased by one fourth.

(33)   What is the correct way to simplify the equation $1 \times 8 \times 8 \times 8 \times 3 \times 3 \times 9$ using exponents?

(A) $1 \times 8^3 \times 3^2 \times 9$

(B) $1 (8 \times 3) (3 \times 2) 9$

(C) $1 \times 8 \times 3 \times 8 \times 2 \times 9$

(D) $1 \times 512 \times 9 \times 9$

(34)   In the number set 12, 14, 19, 22, 24, 36, 78, what is the approximate mean?

(A)   19

(B)   9

(C)   30

(D)   12

(35)   If 25 people enter a drawing for concert tickets and only one person will be selected, what are the chances of any given person's name being drawn?

(A)   1%

(B)   4%

(C)   12%

(D)   25%

(36)   The coach has you and your teammates draw straws to see who will be responsible for cleaning the gym each week. If you have seven teammates, what chance do you have of drawing the short straw?

(A)   1:7

(B)   1:8

(C)   1:9

(D)   1:10

(37)   The roof will cost $4.65 a square foot to re-shingle. If the roof is 240 square feet, how much will it cost to re-shingle?

(A) $111,640

(B) $4.65

(C) $240

(D) $1,116

(38)   There are 30 girls coming to the cheerleader lock-in at the high school. The coach is ordering pizzas for all the girls. If three girls share a pizza, how many pizzas will the coach need to order?

(A)   The coach will need to order 30 pizzas for the girls' lock-in.

(B)   The coach will need to order 15 pizzas for the girls' lock-in.

(C)   The coach will need to order 10 pizzas for the girls' lock-in.

(D)   The coach will need to order 12 pizzas for the girls' lock-in.

Test 1: Reading Comprehension

Directions: Read each passage that follows carefully. Think about the main points, the tone and feel of the passage, the information presented and anything the passage might be implying. When you are through reading each passage, carefully read each question and the corresponding answers. Using the information you gained from the passage, choose the correct answer.

Test 1 Passage 1 & Questions:

1.   Mary, Queen of Scots, is well known for being a rare female monarch
2.   in a world that was almost completely ruled by men,
3.   when most women were still considered property.
4.   She was born prematurely in 1542 at Linlithgow Castle.
5.   She became queen of Scotland six days later, when her father died.
6.   It was first planned that she would marry Prince Edward of England,
7.   but when Scotland refused to change the original marriage alliance, the engagement died.
8.   King Henry VIII tried to force Scotland to give into his demands by waging war with them.
9.   In the middle of all the fighting, a Catholic marriage alliance was made with France.
10.   Mary was sent to live there in 1548 at just six years old
11.   with the intent of her marrying the Dauphin of France, Frances.
12.   They were finally married in 1558 when Mary was sixteen.
13.   In 1560, after the death of Frances' father, Mary became Queen Consort of France,
14.   alongside her husband who became King Frances of France.
15.   Frances died in 1560 of an ear infection, leaving Mary a widow of only eighteen.
16.   Having had no children with Frances, Mary finally returned home to Scotland in 1561.
17.   Scotland was torn by the Catholic-Protestant conflict.
18.   In an attempt to calm things down, she married a Protestant and her second cousin.
19.   Together, she and Henry had one child, a son, James, on June 19, 1566.
20.   Protestants were enraged when Mary baptized her son Catholic.
21.   Her husband died in February 1567.
22.   Mary was forced to step down as queen in favor of her son James in 1567.
23.   She was imprisoned in Leven Castle until her escape in 1568.
24.   Unable to overthrow those in power to reclaim her crown, she fled to England.
25.   There, Queen Elizabeth I used her as a political toy for the next 19 years.
26.   In 1587, Mary was accused and convicted of plotting to have Elizabeth killed.
27.   For the crime, Mary was beheaded at forty-five years old.
28.   Her son James became King of Scotland, England and Ireland in March of 1603,
29.   after the death of Queen Elizabeth, since he was her closest living relative.
30.   James had his mother's body moved in 1612
31.   to a place of honor at Westminster Abbey, where she still resides today.

Directions: Using the passage above, answer each of the five questions that follow. Refer back to the passage to confirm your answer choices and refresh the details of your memory. The answers to all of the questions will either be in the passage or will require your opinion or point of view, so there is no outside information you need to know.

(1) What was the main idea of this passage?

(A) The reign of King James I of England & Ireland.

(B) The reign of King James VI of Scotland.

(C) The reign of Mary, Queen of Scots.

(D) The reign of Queen Elizabeth I of England.

(2) How old was Mary when she became Queen of Scotland?

(A) Mary was sixteen years old.

(B) Mary was six days old.

(C) Mary was six years old.

(D) Mary was eighteen years old.

(3) In what place of honor did James place Mary after her death?

(A) James placed Mary in Linlithgow Castle.

(B) James placed Mary in Westminster Abbey.

(C) James placed Mary in Leven Castle.

(D) None of the above.

(4) What was rare about Mary, Queen of Scots?

(A) She was married at 16 years old.

(B) She was sent to live in another country at age six.

(C) She was a female monarch.

(D) She was married multiple times.

(5)   How long did Queen Elizabeth keep Mary imprisoned before her death?

(A)   Queen Elizabeth kept Mary imprisoned for 19 years.

(B)   Queen Elizabeth kept Mary imprisoned for 16 years.

(C)   Queen Elizabeth kept Mary imprisoned for 2 years.

(D)   Queen Elizabeth kept Mary imprisoned for 6 years.

Test 1 Passage 2 & Questions:

1.   The books we read at home, use in school and check out of the library are all printed.
2.   There was a time, though, when every book was written by hand.
3.   Eventually, wooden block lettering began to be used, which was still done by hand.
4.   It took at least a day for each individual letter to be carved out.
5.   Copying books this way could never be used for any type of large-scale printing
6.   because it took too long and the wooden blocks would wear down over multiple uses.
7.   In order to get a copy of any book, you would have to handwrite the copy
8.   word for word from the original text or letter by letter with block printing.
9.   Either way, the process took a lot of time and effort.
10.   Because of that, books were very expensive to buy and were normally written in Latin.
11.   During this period in time, Latin was almost exclusively spoken, read and written by the wealthy.
12.   In 1439, Johannes Gutenberg invented the first mechanically movable printing press.
13.   His invention used a mechanical press, oil-based ink, a hand mold for creating the word casts,
14.   and mechanical movable type.
15.   The special alloy he created from a combination of metals made the cast extremely durable
16.   against the wear and tear of being used to print multiple works, multiple times.
17.   It also melted at a low temperature and hardened quickly.
18.   His mechanical movable printing press forever changed how books and other texts were made.
19.   It allowed the mass production of books and allowed them to be quickly printed,
20.   copied and distributed.
21.   This was unique because it allowed printing to be done much more inexpensively.
22.   In turn, this gave common people the ability to purchase books as well.
23.   To that end, books were also translated to common languages such as French,
24.   Italian and Greek to name a few at that time.
25.   Gutenberg's invention was said to be a turning point in history,
26.   bringing Europe into the "Age of Enlightenment" and ultimately changing the world forever.
27.   One of the books he is most famous for mass printing is the Gutenberg Bible.
28.   In addition to being an inventor, Johannes Gutenberg was also a blacksmith,

29.	engraver, goldsmith, printer and publisher, all of which contributed to his skill for inventing.

Directions: Using the passage above, answer each of the five questions that follow. Refer back to the passage to confirm your answer choices and refresh the details of your memory. The answers to all of the questions will either be in the passage or will require your opinion or point of view, so there is no outside information you need to know.

(1)	Who was able to afford books before Johannes' invention?

(A)	Everyone could afford books before Johannes' invention.

(B)	Common people could afford books before Johannes' invention.

(C)	Wealthy people could afford books before Johannes' invention.

(D)	People who could read could afford books before Johannes' invention.

(2)	Why was his printing press so important?

(A)	It made books affordable to almost everyone.

(B)	It allowed lots of copies of a book to be made in a short time.

(C)	It was a sustainable way to print books.

(D)	All of the above.

(3)	What were Gutenberg's casts made from?

(A)	Gutenberg's casts were made of a metal alloy.

(B)	Gutenberg's casts were made of gold.

(C)	Gutenberg's casts were made of wood.

(D)	Gutenberg's casts were made of plastic.

(4)	How were most books copied before the mechanical printing press?

(A)	Most books were copied by a copy machine before the printing press.

(B)	Most books were handwritten before the printing press.

(C)	Most books were only written once before the printing press.

(D)	All of the above.

(5)   Why was Johannes Gutenberg's metal alloy so good for printing?

(A)   It melted at a low temperature.

(B)   It cooled and hardened quickly.

(C)   It was durable for repeated use.

(D)   All of the above.

Test 1 Passage 3 & Questions:

1.   Have you ever lain in the cool grass on a clear night and wondered what's out there in the universe?

2.   Well, even if you haven't, a lot of others have, and on October 1, 1958, President Dwight D.

3.   Eisenhower, along with Congress, approved the National Aeronautics and Space Administration

4.   or NASA for short, and announced the birth of Project Mercury on October 7.

5.   Project Mercury was designed to put human-manned spaceships into orbit, circling the earth

6.   to study how humans functioned in space and safely recover astronauts and spaceships.

7.   On April 9, 1959, the Mercury Project introduced the

8.   "Mercury Seven" as the first United States astronauts.

9.   Those seven men were Scott Carpenter, Gordon Cooper, John Glenn Jr., Virgil Grissom,

10.   Walter Schirra Jr., Alan Shepard Jr. and Donald Slayton.

11.   On May 5, 1961, Project Mercury launched its first spaceship, piloted by a human, into space.

12.   Then on February 20, 1962, Project Mercury met its first goal when astronaut John Glenn Jr.

13.   circled the earth three times in Friendship 7 Mercury.

14.   Virgil Grissom operated the first Project Gemini on March 23, 1965.

15.   The second Gemini project happened between June 3rd and June 7th of 1965 when astronaut

16.   Edward White II performed the first spacewalk.

17.   Frank Borman, Jim Lovell and Bill Anders were the first humans to orbit the moon on

18.   December 24, 1968, aboard Apollo 8, almost two years after an accident on Apollo 1 claimed the lives of three American astronauts.

19.   The trip into space that occurred from July 16, 1969 until July 24, 1969 made history around the world. While on this trip, Neil Armstrong and Edward Aldrin Jr. landed Apollo 11 on the

20.   moon's surface, and Neil Armstrong became the first man to walk on the moon.

21.   Over the next decade, NASA and other countries made many space advances. Those advances

22.   led to the successful building of the space shuttle Columbia, which was the first spacecraft to be

23.   able to both take off into orbit and land again, while still having the ability to be reused.

24.   On June 18, 1983, Sally K. Ride made history by becoming the first American female astronaut.

25.   During the April 1990 Discovery space flight, the Hubble Space Telescope was deployed.

26.   The first American female pilot, Eileen Collins, commanded the shuttle Discovery on the

27.   February 1995 space flight in which Discovery passed by the Russian Mir space station.

28.   On July 4, 1997, NASA made history when the Mars Pathfinder landed on Mars,

29.   and released the Sojourner Rover onto its surface two days later. It began sending

30.   pictures from the surface of Mars back to Earth.

31.   Expedition One, the first permanent crew of the International Space Station,

32.   arrived at the space station on November 2, 2002.

33.   Orion, a manned lunar spaceship, was contracted to be built on August 31, 2006.

34.   In December 2006, NASA announced future plans for a permanent settlement on the moon.

35.   Announcements were made on September 12, 2013, that Voyager 1, launched in 1977, had crossed into interstellar space.

36.   In April 2018, the TESS satellite was launched. In July 2019, NASA announced TESS had

37.   located an exoplanet 31 light-years away that might be able to support life.

38.   With so many advances in Earth's study of space, the ends of the universe are literally the limit.

Directions: Using the passage above, answer each of the five questions that follow. Refer back to the passage to confirm your answer choices and refresh the details of your memory. The answers to all of the questions will either be in the passage or will require your opinion or point of view, so there is no outside information you need to know.

(1)   In what year did Project Mercury launch its first shuttle?

(A)   The Mercury Project launched its first shuttle in 1961.

(B)   The Mercury Project launched its first shuttle in 1958.

(C)   The Mercury Project launched its first shuttle in 1959.

(D)   The Mercury Project launched its first shuttle in 1962.

(2)   What spaceship was used in the first human orbit of the moon?

(A)   The first human shuttle to orbit the moon was Friendship 7 Mercury.

(B)   The first human shuttle to orbit the moon was Apollo 8.

(C)   The first human shuttle to orbit the moon was Gemini.

(D)   The first human shuttle to orbit the moon was Apollo 11.

(3)   Who performed the first spacewalk?

(A)   The first spacewalk was performed by Neil Armstrong.

(B)   The first spacewalk was performed by Edward White.

(C)   The first spacewalk was performed by Virgil Grissom.

(D)   The first spacewalk was performed by Jim Lovell.

(4)   Who was the first person to walk on the moon?

(A)   The first person to walk on the moon was Edward Aldrin.

(B)   The first person to walk on the moon was Gordon Cooper.

(C)   The first person to walk on the moon was Neil Armstrong.

(D)   The first person to walk on the moon was John Glenn.

(5)   Who was the first female commander?

(A)   The first American female space commander was Sally K. Ride.

(B)   The first American female space commander was Virgil Grissom.

(C)   The first American female space commander was Eileen Collins.

(D)   The first American female space commander was TESS.

Test 1 Passage 4 & Questions:

1.   The Smithsonian Institute is made up of museums, galleries, gardens and a national zoo.
2.   It is spread out between Washington, D.C. and New York City.
3.   The Washington D.C. sites all offer free admission and are open 364 days a year,
4.   only closing for Christmas Day.
5.   The Smithsonian Institute is made up of 19 different sites, including the African American
6.   Museum; African Art Museum; Air and Space Museum;
7.   Air and Space Museum Udvar-Haze Center; American Art Museum;
8.   American History Museum; American Indian Museum;
9.   American Indian Museum Heye Center; Anacostia Community Museum;
10.   Archives of American Art; Arts and Industries Building; Cooper Hewitt; Freer Gallery of Art;
11.   Hirschhorn; National History Museum; National Portrait Gallery; Postal Museum; Renwick Gallery; S. Dillion Ripley Center; Sackler Gallery; Smithsonian Gardens and the National Zoo.
12.   These total eleven museums, one national zoo, one garden, four galleries, and two other locations. These nineteen locations make up a world-class complex of research and education,
13.   as well as the most comprehensive museums and art galleries worldwide.

Directions: Using the passage above, answer each of the five questions that follow. Refer back to the passage to confirm your answer choices and refresh the details of your memory. The answers to all of the questions will either be in the passage or will require your opinion or point of view, so there is no outside information you need to know.

(1)   How many days a year is the Smithsonian Institute open?

(A)   The Smithsonian Institute and its facilities are open 365 days a year.

(B)   The Smithsonian Institute and its facilities are open 366 days a year.

(C)   The Smithsonian Institute and its facilities are open 364 days a year.

(D)   The Smithsonian Institute and its facilities are open 463 days a year.

(2)   How many places make up the Smithsonian Institute Complex?

(A)   The Smithsonian Institute is made up of nineteen facilities.

(B)   The Smithsonian Institute is made up of eleven facilities.

(C)   The Smithsonian Institute is made up of six facilities.

(D)   The Smithsonian Institute is made up of two facilities.

(3)   Which two locations house the Smithsonian?

(A)   The Smithsonian is located in West Virginia and Washington state.

(B)   The Smithsonian is located in New York and Washington, D.C.

(C)   The Smithsonian is located in Washington and Nashville.

(D)   The Smithsonian is located in Washington and New York.

(4)   What location would have the most information on NASA?

(A)   The most likely place to find NASA information at the Smithsonian is the Air and Space Museum.

(B)   The most likely place to find NASA information at the Smithsonian is the Archives of American Art.

(C)   The most likely place to find NASA information at the Smithsonian is the National History Museum.

(D)   None of the above.

(5)   How much does it cost to go to most of the Smithsonian sites?

(A)   It costs more as you get closer to the White House.

(B)   You must call each location to find out the individual admission fees.

(C)   Admission to the Smithsonian is free.

(D)   None of the above.

Test 1 Passage 5 & Questions:

1.   You sit in a rocking chair on your front porch each day,
2.   waving to the faces that pass by your way.
3.   A smile, a wave or a simple hello,
4.   you never miss a single fellow.
5.   Your gray hair blows in the afternoon breeze.
6.   Your overalls blue,
7.   your T-shirt white,
8.   your bare feet clearly in sight.
9.   Rocking to and rocking fro,
10.   you rock back and forth, nice and slow.
11.   The shade from your porch keeps you cool
12.   and lemonade sweats in a glass beside you on a stool.
13.   As the sun falls low in the sky,
14.   you wave with your last goodbye.
15.   Heading inside when it's nice and cool,
16.   leaving your lemonade out on the stool.
17.   Tomorrow you'll come
18.   and you'll do it again.
19.   For we'd miss you a lot
20.   if you weren't in your spot.

Directions: Using the passage above, answer each of the five questions that follow. Refer back to the passage to confirm your answer choices and refresh the details of your memory. The answers to all of the questions will either be in the passage or will require your opinion or point of view, so there is no outside information you need to know.

(1)   What is the above passage about?

(A)   The passage is about people leaving for work every day.

(B)   The passage is about an old man waving to his neighbors as they come and go.

(C)   The passage is about a kid playing in his neighborhood.

(D)   None of the above.

(2)   What is the meaning of line 12?

(A)   The cold glass of lemonade is wet on the outside of the glass.

(B)   The glass of lemonade smells really bad.

(C)   The lemonade is hot.

(D)   The lemonade is sick.

(3)   What is the man wearing in the passage?

(A)   The man in the passage is wearing overalls and a T-shirt.

(B)   The man in the passage is wearing slacks and a T-shirt.

(C)   The man in the passage is wearing shorts and a T-shirt.

(D)   None of the above.

(4)   What does the passage say would happen if the man wasn't there?

(A)   The passage says that no one would notice if he wasn't there.

(B)   The passage says that he would be forgotten.

(C)   The passage says that it would be like he was never there.

(D)   The passage says that he would be missed.

(5)   When does the man leave his porch?

(A)   The man leaves his porch every morning.

(B)   The man leaves his porch every afternoon when it gets hot.

(C)   The man leaves his porch when the sun sets and it gets cool.

(D)   The man leaves his porch when the moon is out.

Test 1 Mathematics Achievement

Directions: In this Mathematics Achievement practice test you will find a variety of mathematical questions that test your math skills as well as the information you have learned. The questions may include addition, subtraction, multiplication and division, as well as square roots, geometry, measurements, probability and overall problem-solving.

Read each question carefully. Then read each of the multiple-choice questions that follow. Choose the multiple-choice answer that correctly solves each question, word problem or equation. On your official exam, you will be allowed to use the space in your workbook or margins to solve the equations and choose the correct answer. With that in mind, you may use scratch paper to work the equations in this study guide.

(1)   If the values are $p = 25$, $c = 62$, $j = 87$, then what is the solution to the equation: $(p - c)j = $ _____?

(A)   3,219

(B)   -3,219

(C)   32,190

(D)   321,900

(2)   Hillary and Anna have to pick up party supplies at four stores: flowers from Fiona's, decorations from Nel's Décor, a cake from King Kake's and the main entrée from Cole's Catering. It takes 15 minutes to get from their home to Fiona's, 10 minutes to get from Fiona's to Nel's and 45 minutes to get from King Kake's to Cole's Catering. If the girls spent 97 minutes driving, how long did it take them to drive from Nel's to King Kake's?

(A)   It took the girls 16 minutes to get from Nel's to King Kake's.

(B)   It took the girls 27 minutes to get from Nel's to King Kake's.

(C)   It took the girls 34 minutes to get from Nel's to King Kake's.

(D)   It took the girls 55 minutes to get from Nel's to King Kake's.

(3)   What is the square root of 81?

(A)   The square root of 81 is 3.

(B)   The square root of 81 is 9.

(C)   The square root of 81 is 12.

(D)   The square root of 81 is 4.

(4)   What is the most logical equation to find the area of a triangle?

(A)   Area = height multiplied by width

(B)   Area = length multiplied by width

(C)   Area = pi multiplied by the radius squared

(D)   Area = ½(base multiplied by the height)

(5)   145 is the square root of what number?

(A)   145 is the square root of 22,025.

(B)   145 is the square root of 21,025.

(C)   145 is the square root of 24,024.

(D)   145 is the square root of 22,024.

(6)   The GCF of two numbers is 8. If one number is 16 and the other is x, solve for x.

(A) $x = 24$

(B) $x = 12$

(C) $x = 36$

(D) $x = 6$

(7)   What is the square root of 361?

(A)   The square root of 361 is 17.

(B)   The square root of 361 is 18.

(C)   The square root of 361 is 19.

(D)   The square root of 361 is 16.

(8)   Which of the following expresses the number 951,654,002.07 in writing?

(A)   Nine hundred fifty-one million, six hundred fifty-four thousand, two and seven hundredths

(B)   Nine hundred fifty-one thousandths, six hundred fifty-four thousand, two hundred seven

(C)   Nine hundred fifty-one. Six hundred fifty-four. Two and seven-tenths

(D)   Nine five one, six five four, zero zero two, decimal point, zero seven

(9)   Which of the following numerically represents the word problem: fifteen multiplied by twenty-seven increased by seven?

(A) $27 \div 15 - 7$

(B) $15 \times 27 + 7$

(C) $15 + 27 \div 7$

(D) $15 - 27 \times 7$

(10)   In the number 987,687, what place values do the two number 8s hold?

(A)   Ones and tens

(B)   Tens and ten thousands

(C)   Ones and thousands

(D)   Hundreds and hundred-thousands

(11)   Which answer correctly expresses fifty-four and one-fourth?

(A) $\dfrac{54}{1}$

(B) $54\dfrac{1}{4}$

(C) $\dfrac{1}{54}$

(D) $\dfrac{\pi}{2}$

(12) In the number 4876482, what is the place value of the number 6?

(A) Tens

(B) Hundreds

(C) Thousands

(D) Ten thousands

(13) If three-quarters of the ingredients are dry and one-quarter of the ingredients are wet, what percentage of the ingredients are dry?

(A) 30% of the ingredients are dry.

(B) 45% of the ingredients are dry.

(C) 60% of the ingredients are dry.

(D) 75% of the ingredients are dry.

(14) Nine students take the social studies exam. If three students score 90%, two students score 70% and the other four scored 85%, what would the average percentage score be if you rounded to the nearest whole number?

(A) The average percentage score on the social studies exam is 63%.

(B) The average percentage score on the social studies exam is 83%.

(C) The average percentage score on the social studies exam is 73%.

(D) The average percentage score on the social studies exam is 93%.

(15) Heather is packing for her trip to Paris. She is allowed to bring up to three bags weighing no more than five pounds each as part of her airfare. All other bags will be an additional $20 each. Heather has two five-pound bags, three four-pound bags and one 20-pound bag. How much extra money will her luggage cost her?

(A) Heather's luggage will cost her an extra $20.

(B) Heather's luggage will cost her an extra $40.

(C) Heather's luggage will cost her an extra $60.

(D) Heather's luggage will cost her an extra $80.

(16)   Anna wants to buy chocolate-covered strawberries. Small berries are $4.99 each, medium berries are $6.99 each and large berries are $10.99 each. If Anna buys six small berries, eight medium berries and 12 large berries, what will be the total cost?

(A) $217.74.

(B) $161.82.

(C) $187.80.

(D) $227.47.

(17)   Is one million twenty-five thousand six-hundred twenty-three less than or greater than 100,250,623?

(A)   Greater than

(B)   Less than

(C)   Equal to

(D)   It's the absolute value of the number.

(18)   Using $a = 12$, and $c = 37$, complete the calculation: $a + c + 14 =$ ____?

(A)   36

(B)   63

(C)   100

(D)   75

(19)   Chance is the oldest of his siblings. His sister Lilly is 5 and his brother Forest is 13 years younger than he is. Last year Chance was twice as old as Lilly and Forest combined. Chance turned 18 last year. With that in mind, how old are Lilly and Forest?

(A)   Lilly is 4 and Forest is 5.

(B)   Lilly is 5 and Forest is 6.

(C)   Lilly is 6 and Forest is 7.

(D)   Lilly is 5 and Forest is 13.

(20)   Solve for c: $130 - 28 + c = 178$

(A) $c = 76$

(B) $c = -20$

(C) $c = 20$

(D) $c = -76$

(E) $c = 55$

(21)   Round the number 125,698,145.1873 to the nearest thousandth.

(A)   125,698,145.187

(B)   125,698,000.000

(C)   125,700,000.000

(D)   126,000,000.1873

(22)   Write 5,000,000,000 + 900,000,000 + 80,000,000 + 7,000,000 + 600,000+ 50,000+ 4,000 + 300 + 20 + 1 in standard from.

(A)   59,876,543.21

(B)   5,987,654,321

(C) $5 + 9 + 8 + 7 + 6 + 5 + 4 + 3 + 2 + 1$

(D)   598,765,432.10

(23) $14 (7 + 3) - 59 =$?

(A)   81

(B)   98

(C)   35

(D)   91

(24)   362 * 5 + 12 =?

(A)   1,822

(B)   422

(C)   4,344

(D)   3,642

(25)   Ella has $12.42 in her piggy bank. Her mother takes Ella and her two sisters, Penny and Daisy, to the candy shop. Ella shares her piggy-bank money with her sisters. Ella spends $1.27, Penny spends $1.20 and Daisy spends $1.36. How much money does Ella have left?

(A)   Ella has $12.42 left.

(B)   Ella has $8.59 left.

(C)   Ella has $3.83 left.

(D)   Ella has $16.25 left.

(26)   Which numerical expression correctly shows 12^4?

(A) $12 \times 4 = 48$

(B) $12 \times 12 \times 12 \times 12 = 20{,}736$

(C) $4 \times 4 \times 4 \times 4 \times 4 \times 4 \times 4 \times 4 \times 4 \times 4 \times 4 \times 4 = 16{,}777{,}216$

(D) 12^4

(27) Choose the answer that expresses the equation $4^6 + 9^3 + 2^2$ as a word problem.

(A) Four to the sixth power plus nine to the third power plus two to the second power.

(B) Four times six plus nine times three plus two times two

(C) Four plus nine plus two to the eleventh power

(D) Four to the sixth power multiplied by nine to the third power multiplied by two to the second power

(28) Change 15×10^3 into a number.

(A) 1,500

(B) 450

(C) 42,875

(D) 15,000

(29) Solve $\frac{6}{12} + \frac{3}{6} + \frac{9}{24}$ =? and write the answer as a mixed number in lowest terms.

(A) $1\frac{3}{8}$

(B) $\frac{33}{24}$

(C) $1\frac{9}{24}$

(D) $\frac{18}{42}$

(30)   Melody needs 15 feet of fabric to make her new quilt. How many yards of fabric does she need to ask for at the fabric counter?

(A)   Melody needs to ask for 3 yards at the fabric counter.

(B)   Melody needs to ask for 4 yards at the fabric counter.

(C)   Melody needs to ask for 5 yards at the fabric counter.

(D)   Melody needs to ask for 6 yards at the fabric counter.

Test 1 Essay Question

Unlike the other portions of your practice test, there is no right or wrong answer for your essay, so this portion of your practice test will not have an answer section.

Essay Topic

If you could travel to any place in the world, where would you go and why would you want to go there?

Test 1 Answers – Verbal Reasoning

In this Practice Test Answer Key, you will find the correct answer for each of the questions on Practice Test 1. The correct answer will sometimes be followed by an explanation to clarify why that answer is correct.

Test 1 Synonyms   Answers

(1)   The correct answer is: **D) eliminate – to end or get rid of.**

ABOLISH – to end quickly. The answer that has the closest meaning to ABOLISH is **eliminate**.

(2)   The correct answer is: **C) desolate – barren, deserted or fruitless.**

BARREN – fruitless or childless. The answer that has the closest meaning to BARREN is **desolate.**

(3)   The correct answer is: **B) vigilantly – watching carefully.**

CAUTIOUSLY – to proceed with care or be vigilant. The answer that has the closest meaning to CAUTIOUSLY is **vigilantly.**

(4)   The correct answer is: **B) opaque – hard to see through.**

DENSE – heavy, thick, possibly hard to see through. The answer that has the closest meaning to DENSE is **opaque.**

(5)   The correct answer is: **B) elude – to sneakily hide or avoid.**

EVADE – to avoid or hide from. The answer that has the closest meaning to EVADE is **elude.**

(6)   The correct answer is: **A) pointless – hopeless, lacking purpose, in vain.**

FUTILE – lacking value, hopeless, or useless. The answer that has the closest meaning to FUTILE is **pointless.**

(7)   The correct answer is: **D) colossal – very large, impressive or more than life-sized.**

GIGANTIC – huge, very large or massive. The answer that has the closest meaning to GIGANTIC is **colossal.**

(8)   The correct answer is: **C) swindle – to cheat, deceive or defraud.**

HOAX – to deceive or trick. The answer that has the closest meaning to HOAX is **swindle.**

(9)   The correct answer is: **C) duplicate – an identical copy or exact repeat.**

IDENTICAL – exactly the same. The answer that has the closest meaning to IDENTICAL is **duplicate.**

(10)   The correct answer is: **A) cheerful – happy, cheery or fun-loving.**

JOVIAL – cheerful, extremely happy or jolly. The answer that has the closest meaning to JOVIAL is **cheerful.**

(11)   The correct answer is: **D) relations – connected, shared or tied together.**

KIN – family, blood-related, linked. The answer that has the closest meaning to KIN is **relations.**

(12)   The correct answer is: **C) accurate – correct, right or free of errors.**

LITERAL – adhering strictly, word for word, or emphasizing truth. The answer that has the closest meaning to LITERAL is **accurate.**

(13)   The correct answer is: **A) sovereign – self-governing, monarch or with complete power.**

MONARCH – A supreme or very powerful ruler. The answer with the closest meaning to MONARCH is **sovereign.**

(14)   The correct answer is: **B) collaborate – to work together toward a mutual goal.**

NEGOTIATE – to mutually compromise, come to an agreement or strike an alliance. The answer with the closest meaning to NEGOTIATE is **collaborate.**

(15) The correct answer is: **D) topple – to knock over, overthrow or make fall.**

OVERTHROW – to remove abruptly or by force. The answer with the closest meaning to OVERTHROW is **topple.**

(16) The correct answer is: **B) meticulous – extremely detailed or particular.**

PAINSTAKING – great care, attention to detail, scrupulous. The answer with the closest meaning to PAINSTAKING is **meticulous.**

(17) The correct answer is: **A) expedition – to explore the unknown or undertake a journey.**

QUEST – adventurous journey. The answer with the closest meaning to QUEST is **expedition.**

Test 1 Sentence Completion Answers

(1)   The correct answer is: **B) accumulate – to collect, increase, gather or grow.**

The weather report said we are expecting snow and that four to six inches will **accumulate.**

(2)   The correct answer is: **C) briskly – to move quickly or with vigor.**

I walk **briskly** through the park because it is so cold.

(3)   The correct answer is: **D) construct – to put together or build.**

I used my father's tools and lumber to **construct** my project for social studies.

(4)   The correct answer is: **A) dissatisfied – frustrated, unhappy or discontent.**

The customer was **dissatisfied** with the broken television he received.

(5)   The correct answer is: **B) she always exaggerated the truth.**

No one believed Evelyn's stories because **she always exaggerated the truth**.

(6)   The correct answer is: **C) it was frigid outside.**

I needed a winter coat, gloves and boots because **it was frigid outside**.

Explanation: Balmy outside and sweltering outside both refer to the weather being hot; brisk outside could possibly be the answer since brisk refers to chilly. However, frigid refers to being extremely cold, and the sentence indicates that its extremely cold because of the need for a winter coat, gloves and boots.

(7)   The correct answer is: **D) genuinely – real, candid or sincerely.**

I was **genuinely** excited to go to the carnival with my family.

(8)   The correct answer is: **A) heroic – brave or courageous.**

The knight was absolutely **heroic** when he charged the dragon with his sword drawn to save the damsel.

(9)   The correct answer is: **B) irrigate – supply with water, wash out or refresh.**

The cut was deep, so the doctor had to **irrigate** the wound before closing it.

(10)   The correct answer is: **C) horizontally – parallel to the horizon or level.**

The horizon runs **horizontally** along the bay.

(11)   The correct answer is: **D) leisure – fun or relaxing activities.**

In my **leisure** time, I enjoy reading, painting and dancing.

(12)   The correct answer is: **A) moral – personal conscience, standard of justice, ethical, or honorable.**

It went against my **moral** judgment to steal the rival school's mascot.

(13)   The correct answer is: **B) well-known myths of all time.**

The Greek gods are some of the most **well-known myths of all time.**

(14) The correct answer is: **C) oblivious – unaware, ignorant or unmindful.**

Connie was so engrossed in her novel that she was **oblivious** to everything going on around her.

(15) The correct answer is: **D) portable – easily movable, transportable, convenient.**

The best place in the city to see the stars is the top of Mount Olive, but you need a **portable** telescope to take there.

(16) The correct answer is: **A) quote – repeat someone's exact words, exact reference, estimate.**

The body shop gave me a **quote** for the cost of repairs.

(17) The correct answer is: **A) to – preposition indicating direction, destination or position, or word used before the infinitive form of a verb.**

My little sister was so excited **to** go for ice cream that she wore herself out and fell asleep before we arrived.

Explanation: Answer B, too, means also and answer C, two, refers to the number 2.

Test 1 Answers – Quantitative Reasoning

(1)   The correct answer is: **B) *b* = number of bells needed ÷ number of bells in each bag.**

(2)   The correct answer is: **B) (*f* + *s* + *t*) ÷ 3 = the average points per game.**

EXPLANATION: To find the average of a set of numbers, add the value of each number in the set together. Then divide the sum by the number of numbers in the set. In this case, 12 + 10 + 22 = 44, so Philip scored a total of 44 points between the three games. 44 ÷ 3 = 14.67. You could round the average to the nearest whole number, so Philip's average points per game would be 15.

(3)   The correct answer is: **D) Grapes, Oranges, Bananas, Apples.**

EXPLANATION: According to the chart, there are 30 oranges, 10 apples, 40 grapes and 20 bananas. Therefore, in the order of most sales to least, that is 40 grapes, 30 oranges, 20 bananas and 10 apples.

(4)   The correct answer is: **C) Jessica will need 3 boxes of tea for her trip.**

EXPLANATION: Jessica drinks a cup of tea a day. She will be gone for 14 days. This means she will use 14 tea bags in total. If one box of tea has 5 tea bags, she will need at least 3 boxes of tea to take on her trip (5 + 5 = 10 + 5 = 15).

(5)   The correct answer is: **B) The basketball team.**

EXPLANATION: Out of the four sports teams listed, football and soccer have the most team members with 16 teammates each. The volleyball team and cheer squad have 12 team members each, and finally the basketball team has the least with only 8 team members.

(6)   The correct answer is: **C) Wall C.**

EXPLANATION: The length of the painting is 29 inches long. So the wall must be at least as long as the painting for it to fit. Wall A and Wall B are each too short because they are 24 inches and 12 inches long respectively. Wall A is 5 inches too short and Wall B is 12 inches too short. Wall C is 12 inches longer than the painting; therefore, the painting will fit on Wall C.

(7)   The correct answer is: **B) Pounds.**

(8)   The correct answer is: **A) 7 students are out sick.**

EXPLANATION: There are 24 students in the class. To find the solution to 30% of 24 based on your answer options, turn the percentage into a decimal (30% = 0.30). Multiply the decimal value of the percentage by the whole number you are trying to find the percentage for ($0.3 \times 24 = 7.2$). Because the question is not asking you for an exact number, and based on the options given, it is reasonable to choose A as the answer since 7 is the closest whole number to the actual answer of 7.2.

(9)   The correct answer is: **A) -32 + 90 = 58.**

EXPLANATION: The word problem asks you to choose the correct answer for the sum of -32 and 90. This indicates that you add the two numbers. You can eliminate answer B since it is multiplication. Answer C can logically be eliminated because the number 32 is positive and the answer should be 58, not 90. Finally, answer D can be eliminated because it is a subtraction. Therefore, the logical answer you are left with is A.

(10)   The correct answer is: **A) The middle of a set of numbers when placed in order.**

EXPLANATION: By definition, the median is the middle number of an ordered pattern. For example, if you had the number set: 3, 6, 9, 12, 15, 18, 21, the median would be the number 12 because it falls exactly in the middle of the set of numbers.

(11)   The correct answer is: **B) 9.**

EXPLANATION: To find the median you first must arrange the data in order from least to greatest. This set of data would be arranged 3, 4, 9, 11, 16. The median is the middle number of the set, which is 9.

(12)   The correct answer is: **A) ½(base × height) = Area.**

EXPLANATION: To find the area of a triangle, take the base and multiply this by the perpendicular height (the measure at 90 degrees from the base to the highest point of the triangle). Then find one half of your answer.

(13)   The correct answer is: **C) Denominator.**

EXPLANATION: There are two parts to a common fraction. The top number is the numerator and the bottom number is the denominator. Answer A can be eliminated because it is the top number of a fraction. Answer B can be eliminated because a mixed number is a whole number and a fraction expressed together. And answer D can be eliminated because a whole number is not a fraction.

(14)   The correct answer is: **A) Miles per hour.**

EXPLANATION: Speed, like that of a car, is measured by the number of miles that can be driven in an hour. Answer options B, C and D are generally used to measure the length of something but refer to the length of an object or the distance between objects. Miles, on the other hand, are used to measure how quickly an object (such as a car or train) takes to go from point A to point B.

(15)   The correct answer is: **C) Do the calculations in parentheses first.**

EXPLANATION: The first step you take to solve an equation with multiple operations is to start with the calculations in parentheses: $(4 + 9 - 3) (8 + 8) = (13 - 3) (16) = (10) (16)$. Then work the multiplication and division in the equation: $1 + 6 (10) (16) - 12 = 1 + 6 \times 160 - 12 = 1 + 960 - 12$. Finally, work the addition and subtraction in the order that they appear: $961 - 12 = 949$.

(16)   The correct answer is: **D) Greater than.**

EXPLANATION: The elephant weighs 10 tons; the hippo weighs 8 tons. 10 tons is > 8 tons, so the elephant's weight is greater than the hippo's.

(17)   The correct answer is: **B) 300 + 10 + 5.**

EXPLANATION: Expanded form means to separate the given number by each individual place value and use each value in an equation that adds up to the whole value. So the number 315 in expanded form is 300 + 10 + 5 = 315.

(18)   The correct answer is: **A) It will cost about $145 to make the trip.**

EXPLANATION: The semitruck can drive 15 miles for every 1 gallon of gas (15:1 ratio). The truck is driving a total of 675 miles. To find the cost of fuel for the trip, divide the total miles (675) by the number of miles the truck gets per gallon (15) and multiply the total by the cost of fuel per gallon ($3.25), so 675 ÷ 15 = 45 × $3.25 = $146.25.

(19)   The correct answer is: **C) Approximately 450 apples.**

EXPLANATION: To find the answer you take the number of pies Avery will make for a day (30) and multiply it by the number of apples each pie uses (15), so 30 × 15 = 450.

(20)   The correct answer is: **A) 2.**

EXPLANATION: The Greatest Common Factor of 224, 682 and 348 is 2. 224, 682 and 348 can all be divided by 2 to give a whole number answer. If we take the factor of 12, 224 will not divide by 12 to give a whole number answer. If it does not divide by 12, we know it will not divide by 24 or 48 either, as these are multiples of 12. If 12, 24 and 48 are not factors of 224, they cannot be common factors between all three numbers. They can therefore be eliminated, to leave 2 as the Greatest Common Factor.

(21)   The correct answer is: **D) 56.**

EXPLANATION: The Least Common Multiple of 7, 14 and 56 is 56. This is because 56 is the lowest number in all the times tables of 7, 14 and 56.

(22)   The correct answer is: **D) 163 and 3.**

EXPLANATION: When multiplied together, the lowest factors will equal the number you are factoring. $163 \times 3 = 489$.

(23)   The correct answer is: **A) 2.**

EXPLANATION: Answers B, C and D are not prime numbers. They are even numbers and multiples of two, but answer option A is the only prime number, as it is not a multiple of any number except 1.

(24)   The correct answer is: **C) 37.**

(25)   The correct answer is: **C) 144.**

(26)   The correct answer is: **D) 345.**

(27)   The correct answer is: **A) 1/5 – 5/10 + 10/15.**

(28)   The correct answer is: **A) 70.**

EXPLANATION: The LCD is the Lowest Common Denominator. The denominator is the bottom number of a fraction. In order to do this, you should reduce the fractions first, and then convert the denominators so they are all the same. The first fraction 12/14 reduces to 6/7. The second fraction 10/25 reduces to 2/5, and the third fraction 8/16 reduces to 1/2. The denominators are now 7, 5, and 2, which have an LCD of (7 x 5 x 2) or 70.

(29)   The correct answer is: **B) 1, 2 and 4.**

(30)   The correct answer is: **A) For every five vanilla cookies, there is one chocolate cookie.**

(31)   The correct answer is: **A) The absolute value of x and j.**

EXPLANATION: The vertical line on either side of the equation $x + j$ means the absolute value of the equation.

(32)   The correct answer is: **A) One fourth increased by twelve and three-eighths multiplied by six squared.**

(33)   The correct answer is: **A) $1 \times 8^3 \times 3^2 \times 9$.**

EXPLANATION: To convert an equation using exponents you take the numbers that are repeated ($8 \times 8 \times 8$) and convert it to 8^3. Do the same thing with the other repeated values. This allows you to simplify the equation.

(34)   The correct answer is: **C) 30.**

EXPLANATION: To find the mean of a number set, add the value of each number in the set together (12 + 14 + 19 + 22 + 24 + 36 + 78 = 205) and then divide the sum by the number of numbers in the set (205 ÷ 7 = 29.3). For this equation, choose the answer option that is closest to the value of the mean.

(35)   The correct answer is: **B) 4%.**

EXPLANATION: To find the percentage, divide 100 by the whole number you are wanting to find the percentage for. In this case, 100 ÷ 25 = 4; therefore, each person represents 4% of the total group.

(36)   The correct answer is: **B) 1:8.**

EXPLANATION: There are 8 teammates. So each player has a 1 in 8 chance of drawing the short straw.

(37)   The correct answer is: **D) $1,116.**

EXPLANATION: To solve this equation, multiply the square footage of the roof (240 square feet) by the cost per square foot to re-shingle ($4.65) to find the total $1,116.

(38)   The correct answer is: **C) The coach will need to order 10 pizzas for the girls' lock-in.**

EXPLANATION: Divide the number of girls (30) by the number that can each share a pizza (3) to find the number of pizzas that will need to be ordered, so 30 ÷ 3 = 10.

Test 1 Answers: Reading Comprehension

Test 1 Passage 1 – Answers

This passage describes the life of Mary, Queen of Scots: how she became queen, her life as queen and her eventual death, as well as how she was posthumously honored by her son.

(1)   The correct answer is: **C) The reign of Mary, Queen of Scots.**

QUESTION: What was the main idea of this passage?

EXPLANATION: This answer can be found in lines 1 and 5: "Mary, Queen of Scots, ... She became Queen of Scotland six days later, when her father died."

(2)   The correct answer is: **B) Mary was six days old.**

QUESTION: How old was Mary when she became Queen of Scotland?

EXPLANATION: This answer can be found in line 5: "She became Queen of Scotland six days later, when her father died."

(3)   The correct answer is: **B) James placed Mary in Westminster Abbey.**

QUESTION: In what place of honor did James place Mary after her death?

EXPLANATION: This answer can be found in lines 30-31: "James had his mother's body moved in 1612 to a place of honor at Westminster Abbey where she still resides today."

(4)   The correct answer is: **C) She was a female monarch.**

QUESTION: What was rare about Mary, Queen of Scots?

EXPLANATION: This answer can be found in lines 1-2: "Mary, Queen of Scots, is well known for being a rare female monarch in a world that was almost completely ruled by men, when most women were still considered property."

(5)   The correct answer is: **A) Queen Elizabeth kept Mary prisoner for 19 years.**

QUESTION: How long did Queen Elizabeth keep Mary imprisoned before her death?

EXPLANATION: This answer can be found in lines 24-25: "Unable to overthrow those in power to reclaim her crown, she fled to England. There, Queen Elizabeth I used her as a political toy for the next 19 years."

Test 1 Passage 2 – Answers

This passage is about Johannes Gutenberg and his invention of the mechanical printing press, as well as how his invention changed books and printing forever.

(1)   The correct answer is: **C) Wealthy people could afford books before Johannes' invention.**

QUESTION: Who was able to afford books before Johannes' invention?

EXPLANATION: This answer can be found in line 10: "Because of that, books were very expensive to buy…"

(2)   The correct answer is: **D) All of the above.**

QUESTION: Why was his printing press so important?

EXPLANATION: This answer can be found in lines 18-20: "His mechanical moveable printing press forever changed how books and other texts were made. It allowed the mass production of books and allowed them to be quickly printed, copied and distributed."

(3)   The correct answer is: **A) Gutenberg's casts were made of a metal alloy.**

QUESTION: What were Gutenberg's casts made from?

EXPLANATION: This answer can be found in lines 15-16: "The special alloy he created from a combination of metals made the cast extremely durable against the wear and tear of being used to print multiple works, multiple times."

(4)   The correct answer is: **B) Most books were handwritten before the printing press.**

QUESTION: How were most books copied before the mechanical printing press?

EXPLANATION: This answer can be found in lines 7-8: "In order to get a copy of any book, you would have to handwrite the copy word for word from the original text or letter by letter with block printing."

(5)   The correct answer is: **D) All of the above.**

QUESTION: Why was Johannes Gutenberg's metal alloy so good for printing?

EXPLANATION: This answer can be found in lines 15-17: "The special alloy he created from a combination of metals made the cast extremely durable against the wear and tear of being used to print multiple works, multiple times. It also melted at a low temperature and hardened quickly."

Test 1 Passage 3 – Answers

This passage is about the creation and evolution of NASA, its explorations and its discoveries.

(1)   The correct answer is: **A) The Mercury Project launched its first shuttle in 1961.**

QUESTION: In what year did Project Mercury launch its first shuttle?

EXPLANATION: The answer to this question can be found in line 11: "On May 5, 1961, Project Mercury launched its first spaceship, piloted by a human, into space."

(2)   The correct answer is: **B) The first human shuttle to orbit the moon was Apollo 8.**

QUESTION: What spaceship was used in the first human orbit of the moon?

EXPLANATION: The answer can be found in lines 17-18: "Frank Borman, Jim Lovell and Bill Anders were the first humans to orbit the moon on December 24, 1968, aboard Apollo 8."

(3)   The correct answer is: **B) The first spacewalk was performed by Edward White.**

QUESTION: Who performed the first spacewalk?

EXPLANATION: The answer can be found in line 16: "Edward White II performed the first spacewalk."

(4)   The correct answer is: **C) The first person to walk on the moon was Neil Armstrong.**

QUESTION: Who was the first person to walk on the moon?

EXPLANATION: The answer can be found in line 20: "...Neil Armstrong because the first man to walk on the moon."

(5)   The correct answer is: **C) The first American female commander was Eileen Collins.**

QUESTION: Who was the first female astronaut commander?

EXPLANATION: The answer can be found in line 26: "The first American female pilot, Eileen Collin, commanded the shuttle Discovery."

Test 1 Passage 4 – Answers

This passage is about the Smithsonian Institute and its museums, galleries, gardens and zoo.

(1)   The correct answer is: **C) The Smithsonian Institute and its facilities are open 364 days a year.**

QUESTION: How many days a year is the Smithsonian Institute open?

EXPLANATION: The answer can be found in line 3: "The Washington D.C. sites all offer free admission and are open 364 days a year."

(2)   The correct answer is: **A) The Smithsonian is made up of 19 facilities.**

QUESTION: How many places make up the Smithsonian Institute Complex?

EXPLANATION: The answer can be found in line 5: "The Smithsonian Institute is made up of 19 different sites."

(3)   The correct answer is: **B) The Smithsonian is located in New York and Washington, D.C.**

QUESTION: Which two locations house the Smithsonian?

EXPLANATION: The answer and its support can be found in lines 1-2: "The Smithsonian Institute is made up of museums, galleries, gardens and a national zoo. It is spread out between Washington, D.C. and New York City."

(4)   The correct answer is: **A) The most likely place to find NASA information at the Smithsonian is the Air and Space Museum.**

QUESTION: What location would have the most information on NASA?

EXPLANATION: The answer to this question is an assumption based on the names of some of the Smithsonian facilities.

(5)   The correct answer is: **C) Admission to the Smithsonian is free.**

QUESTION: How much does it cost to go to most of the Smithsonian sites?

EXPLANATION: The answer to this question can be found in line 3: "The Washington D.C. sites all offer free admission and are open 364 days a year."

<u>Test 1 Passage 5 – Answers</u>

(1)   The correct answer is: **B) The passage is about an old man waving to his neighbors as they come and go.**

QUESTION: What is the above passage about?

EXPLANATION: The answer to this question can be concluded from lines 2-5: "Waving to the faces that pass by your way; A smile, a wave or a simple hello, you never miss a single fellow. Your gray hair blows in the afternoon breeze."

(2)   The correct answer is: **A) The cold glass of lemonade is wet on the outside of the glass.**

QUESTION: What is the meaning of line 12?

EXPLANATION: Line 12 reads "and lemonade sweats in a glass beside you on a stool." A glass "sweats" when its contents are cold and the air around it is very warm.

(3)   The correct answer is: **A) The man in the passage is wearing overalls and a T-shirt.**

QUESTION: What is the man wearing in the passage?

EXPLANATION: The answer can be found in lines 6-8: "Your overalls blue, your T-shirt white, your bare feet clearly in sight."

(4)   The correct answer is: **D) The passage says that he would be missed.**

QUESTION: What does the passage say would happen if the man wasn't there?

EXPLANATION: The answer to this question can be found in lines 19-20: "For we'd miss you a lot if you weren't in your spot."

(5)   The correct answer is: **C) The man leaves his porch when the sun sets and it gets cool.**

QUESTION: When does the man leave his porch?

EXPLANATION: The answer can be found in lines 13-15: "As the sun falls low in the sky, you wave with your last goodbye. Heading inside when it's nice and cool."

Test 1 Mathematics Achievement

(1)   The correct answer is: **B) -3,219.**

EXPLANATION: p is 25, c is 62 and j is 87. The first step is to complete the equation in parentheses: $(25 - 62) \, 87 = ?$ The result of 25 minus 62 is -37: $(25 - 62) = -37$. The result of 37 multiplied by 87 is -3,219: $-37 \times 87 = -3,219$.

(2)   The correct answer is: **B) It took the girls 27 minutes to get from Nel's to King Kake's.**

EXPLANATION: The whole trip took Hillary and Anna 97 minutes. 97 minutes minus 15 minutes from home to Fiona's, 10 minutes from Fiona's to Nel's, and 45 minutes from King's to Cole's leaves 27 minutes.

(3)   The correct answer is: **B) The square root of 81 is 9.**

EXPLANATION: 9×9 is 81. Therefore, the square root of 81 is 9.

(4)   The correct answer is: **D) Area = ½ (base multiplied by the height).**

EXPLANATION: To find the area of a triangle you take half of the product of the base and height. The base and height are the two sides of the triangle that create the right angle in a right triangle.

(5)   The correct answer is: **B) 145 is the square root of 21,025.**

EXPLANATION: 145 multiplied by 145 is 21,025. Therefore, the square root of 21,025 is 145.

(6)   The correct answer is: **A) $x = 24$.**

(7)   The correct answer is: **C) The square root of 361 is 19.**

EXPLANATION: The square root of 361 is 19. 19 multiplied by 19 is 361.

(8) The correct answer is **A) Nine hundred fifty-one million, six hundred fifty-four thousand, two and seven hundredths.**

(9)   The correct answer is: **B) 15 × 27 + 7.**

(10)   The correct answer is: **B) Ten and ten thousands.**

(11)   The correct answer is: **B) $54\frac{1}{4}$.**

(12)   The correct answer is: **C) Thousands.**

(13)   The correct answer is: **D) 75% of the ingredients are dry.**

EXPLANATION: The equation is easily split into four equal parts: three parts dry and one part wet. In four parts you can divide the total percentage (100%) into sections of 25%. So if 3 parts are dry, 25% + 25% + 25% = 75% are dry ingredients.

(14)   The correct answer is: **B) The average percentage score for the social studies exam is 83%.**

EXPLANATION: To find the average of the social studies percentage scores, multiply the number of tests that scored the same percentage together (70% × 2, 90% × 3, and 85% × 4). Add the total of the scores together (750) and divide that number by the total number of tests taken. 750 ÷ 9 = 83.333. Rounding to the nearest whole number, 83% is the average score for the social studies test.

(15)   The correct answer is: **C) Heather's luggage will cost her an extra $60.**

EXPLANATION: Heather is allowed three bags of five pounds or less as part of her fare. So her three, four-pound bags are included in her fare. The three additional bags will cost $20 each and 20 × 3 = 60, so the three additional bags will cost Heather $60.

(16)   The correct answer is: **A) $217.74.**

EXPLANATION: 6 × $4.99 = $29.94; 8 × $6.99 = $55.92; 12 × $10.99 = $131.88.

The sum of the bunches of berries is $29.94 + $55.92 + $131.88 = $217.74.

(17)   The correct answer is: **B) Less than.**

EXPLANATION: 1,025,623 is less than 100,250,623.

(18)   The correct answer is: **B) 63**

EXPLANATION: $a + c + 14 = ?$ Putting the values into the equation, we get 12 + 37 + 14 = ? So 12 + 37 = 49 and 49 + 14 = 63.

(19)   The correct answer is: **B) Lilly is 5 and Forest is 6.**

EXPLANATION: Chance was 18 one year ago, so he is 19 years old now. Last year Lilly and Forest's combined age multiplied by two was Chance's age. So if Chance was 18 last year, 18 divided by 2 is nine. You know Lilly is five this year so she was four last year. So 9 − 4 = 5, meaning Forest was five last year. Forrest is six this year. You know this for sure because the question states he is 13 years younger than Chance, and 19 − 13 is 6.

(20)   The correct answer is: **A) $c = 76$.**

EXPLANATION: To solve this equation you work the problem in reverse to find c. 178 − 130 + 28 = c. 178 − 130 = 48 + 28 = 76.

(21)   The correct answer is: **A) 125,698,145.187.**

EXPLANATION: The thousandths place is the third number to the right of the decimal point. Rule of rounding: 0 through 4 round down; 5 through 9 round up. The number in the ten-thousandths place is a 3, so you will round down.

(22)   The correct answer is: **B) 5,987,654,321.**

(23)   The correct answer is: **A) 81.**

EXPLANATION: Solve the equations in parentheses first: $(7 + 3) = 10$. Next, multiply: $14 (10) = 140$. Finally, subtract: $140 - 59 = 81$.

(24)   The correct answer is: **A) 1,822.**

EXPLANATION: Start by performing the multiplication: $362 \times 5 = 1,810$. Then perform the addition: $1,810 + 12 = 1,822$.

(25)   The correct answer is: **B) Ella has \$8.59 left.**

EXPLANATION: Ella has \$12.42 in her piggy bank. Ella spent \$1.27, Penny spent \$1.20 and Daisy spent \$1.36. The girls spent a total of \$3.83. If Ella started with \$12.42 and spent \$3.83, she has \$8.95 left.

(26)   The correct answer is **B) $12 \times 12 \times 12 \times 12 = 20,736$.**

EXPLANATION: 12 to the 4th power means multiplying 12 by itself four times.

(27)   The correct answer is **A) Four to the sixth power plus nine to the third power plus two to the second power.**

(28)   The correct answer is: **D) 15,000.**

EXPLANATION: $10^3 = 10 \times 10 \times 10 = 1{,}000$. 15 multiplied by 1,000 is 15,000.

(29)   The correct answer is: **A) $1\frac{3}{8}$**

EXPLANATION: The first step is to make your fractions all have the same denominator. 12, 6 and 24 have the common denominator of 24. $\frac{12}{24} + \frac{12}{24} + \frac{9}{24} = \frac{33}{24}$. Convert your fraction to a mixed number. 24 goes into 33 once with 9 left over. The mixed number becomes $1\frac{9}{24}$. Finally, put the fraction of your mixed number into lowest terms, so $1\frac{9}{24} = 1\frac{3}{8}$

(30)   The correct answer is: **C) Melody needs to ask for 5 yards at the fabric counter.**

EXPLANATION: There are 3 feet in 1 yard. If Melody needs 15 feet of fabric, divide 15 by 3 to give 5. Melody needs 5 yards of fabric for her quilt.

Test 2: Verbal Reasoning

In the Verbal Reasoning section of this practice test, you will find practice questions that require you to do one of two things. You will either choose the **synonym** that means the same or similar thing to the **CAPITALIZED** word beside each numbered question, or you will be asked to choose from the multiple-choice answers to select the word or phrase that most logically **completes the sentence** you're given.

Synonym Directions: For the following practice test questions, read the **CAPITALIZED** word carefully. Choose the multiple-choice answer that means the same or close to the same as the **CAPITALIZED** word.

(1)   RETIRE

(A)   work

(B)   withdraw

(C)   surge

(D)   exchange

(2)   SALVAGE

(A)   rubbish

(B)   disheveled

(C)   reclaim

(D)   toss

(3)   THRIFTY

(A)   frugal

(B)   careless

(C)   uneconomical

(D)   reverent

(4)   UNANIMOUS

(A)   uncommon

(B)   disagreement

(C)   divided

(D)   undisputed

(5)   VISIBLE

(A)   indiscernible

(B)   invisible

(C)   unperceivable

(D)   obvious

(6)   WITHDRAW

(A)   extract

(B)   advance

(C)   remain

(D)   join

(7)   AGGRESSIVE

(A)   peaceful

(B)   compromising

(C)   belligerent

(D)   compelling

(8)   BOISTEROUS

(A)   inactive

(B)   unruly

(C)   placid

(D)   benevolent

(9)   CHALLENGE

(A)   comply

(B)   unopposed

(C)   undisputed

(D)   confront

(10)   DEPLETE

(A)   abundance

(B)   increase

(C)   bountiful

(D)   exhaust

(11)   EXASPERATE

(A)   infuriate

(B)   congealed

(C)   placate

(D)   endure

(12)   FUSE

(A)   repel

(B)   conjure

(C)   mingle

(D)   separate

(13)   GORGE

(A)   nibble

(B)   gluttonous

(C)   starve

(D)   purge

(14) HABITAT

(A) vessel

(B) containment

(C) surge

(D) locale

(15) ILLUMINATE

(A) confuse

(B) darken

(C) illumine

(D) estrange

(16) KNACK

(A) talent

(B) incapable

(C) unable

(D) stunted

(17) LUXURIOUS

(A) uncomfortable

(B) deluxe

(C) unpleasant

(D) meager

Sentence Completion Directions: For the following practice test questions, choose the answer that logically completes each sentence. Then read the question to yourself again with the answer you've chosen to ensure that it still makes sense to you, before moving on to the next one.

Test 2 Sentence Completion

(1)   Completing 400 orders by the end of the day was completely ____.

(A)   hopeful

(B)   unrealistic

(C)   predictable

(D)   condoning

(2)   The rooftops of the houses were covered in ____ panels.

(A)   locking

(B)   dowdy

(C)   solar

(D)   lunar

(3)   The baby was crying frantically and ____.

(A)   would not persevere.

(B)   would not be overwhelmed.

(C)   would not be soothed.

(D)   would not persist.

(4)   The Ferris wheel was ____ and overshadowed all of the other carnival rides.

(A)   minuscule

(B)   nanoscopic

(C)   standard

(D)   massive

(5)   The GPS was supposed to help my father to ____ to our destination, but he didn't use it.

(A)   navigate

(B)   steer

(C)   wander

(D)   stray

(6)   The course had a lot of ____ that we had to evade in order to reach the finish line.

(A)   incentives

(B)   obstacles

(C)   unencumbered

(D)   reluctant

(7)   There was a secret ____ behind the tapestry in the hall.

(A)   partition

(B)   obstruction

(C)   passage

(D)   occlusion

(8)   There was a/an ____ of food after the harvest, so we shared the bounty.

(A)   scarcity

(B)   dearth

(C)   scantiness

(D)   abundance

(9)   Coke, lemonade, coffee, tea and water are the ____ offered at the restaurant.

(A)   beverages

(B)   condiments

(C)   sustenance

(D)   rations

(10)   My dad got Charlie, a 75-pound mastiff, as a/an ____ so he wouldn't be alone anymore.

(A)   opponent

(B)   companion

(C)   antagonist

(D)   discord

(11)   I wanted to have a clone, so I ____ myself to get one.

(A)   cloned

(B)   duplicated

(C)   paralleled

(D)   coupled

(12)   I was feeling diminished after ____.

(A)   my boss told me I had done a superb job.

(B)   my boss told me I had done a superlative job.

(C)   my boss told me I had done an inferior job.

(D)   my boss told me I had done a competent job.

(13)   The fruit in the basket were in fact wax and completely ____.

(A)   palatable

(B)   edible

(C)   rancid

(D)   inedible

(14)   The chocolate had melted and the chocolate-covered strawberries were ____ together.

(A)   fused

(B)   independent

(C)   sundered

(D)   dispirited

(15)   The sun through my office window left a horrible ____ on my computer screen.

(A)   shadow

(B)   glare

(C)   reflection

(D)   silhouette

(16)   If we do not remember our ____, we are doomed to repeat it.

(A)   future

(B)   hereafter

(C)   history

(D)   premonition

(17)   As we approached the pier, Sarah pointed to her favorite ride and squealed, "____"

(A)   Their it is!

(B)   They're it is!

(C)   There it is!

(D)   None of the above.

Test 2: Quantitative Reasoning

Directions: In this section, you will find a variety of questions that test your quantitative reasoning skills. The questions in this section will involve a variety of mathematical skills including mathematical operations, measurements, probability, logical reasoning and more. You will be provided with additional information such as graphs or shapes if they are needed for a specific question.

Read each of the questions and answers carefully. If unsure, consider what information is provided with each possible answer. Eliminate the answers you know don't fit until you reach the most logical answer.

(1)   The horses get 2 cups of grain and 1 cup of oats each morning. If there are 8 horses, how will David figure out how many cups of grain *(g)* and oats *(o)* to use?

(A) $2(g) + 1(o)$

(B)   number of horses $\times (2(g) + 1(o))$

(C)   (number of horses $\times 2g$) + (number of horses + o) = cups of grain and cups of oats

(D) $8(g + o)$

(2)   Anna drove to the movies in Gatesville. It cost her $84 in gas for the round trip and she had to fill up her tank once each way. What equation would you use to figure out how much one tank *(t)* of gas was?

(A) $\$84 \div 2 = t$

(B) $t = \$84 \times 2$

(C) $\$84 - 2 = t$

(D) $t - 2 = \$84$

(3)   What is the symbol for the mathematical constant pi 3.14159?

(A) $\cong$

(B) $\dfrac{\pi}{2}$

(C) $\neq$

(D) π

(4)   Based on the chart, what two years were best for Justin's sales?

(A)   Justin had his best sales in 2019 and 2018.

(B)   Justin had his best sales in 2016 and 2017.

(C)   Justin had his best sales in 2017 and 2018.

(D)   Justin had his best sales in 2017 and 2019.

(5)   Brian is building a new paddock for his horses. If the paddock has four sides, two sides that are congruent, and two of which are congruent and longer than the original two, what shape is the paddock?

(A)   The paddock will be in the shape of a triangle.

(B)   The paddock will be in the shape of a rectangle.

(C)   The paddock will be in the shape of a diamond.

(D)   The paddock will be in the shape of a square.

(6)   The parking lot has 19 spaces. Six spaces are for full-size SUVs, six spaces are for economy vehicles, the two up front are for electric cars and the rest are for compact cars. How many spaces are there for compact cars?

(A)   There are 6 spaces for compact cars.

(B)   There are 5 spaces for compact cars.

(C)   There are 7 spaces for compact cars.

(D)   There are 4 spaces for compact cars.

(7)   There are six lemur enclosures and 27 lemurs at the zoo. If there are four lemurs in each of the first five enclosures, how many lemurs are in the sixth?

(A)   There are 7 lemurs in the last enclosure.

(B)   There are 6 lemurs in the last enclosure.

(C)   There are 4 lemurs in the last enclosure.

(D)   There are 5 lemurs in the last enclosure.

(8)   Martha runs around the park twice a day. What is the best way to measure the length of her runs?

(A)   Feet

(B)   Millimeters

(C)   Pints

(D)   Miles

(9)   Which of the equations shows twenty-five is less than forty-five?

(A) $25 = 45$

(B) $25 > 45$

(C) $25 < 45$

(D) $25/45$

(10)   Annabel the whale is being seen by the vet today. Which unit of measurement would most likely be used to measure her weight?

(A)   Ounces

(B)   Pints

(C)   Quarts

(D)   Tons

(11)   Markus and his family own an apple orchard. When harvest season starts, they sell their apples for $10 a _____.

(A)   Quart

(B)   Bushel

(C)   Pint

(D)   Gallon

(12)   Mason's house sits on 522,720 square feet of land. If an acre is 43,506 square feet, Mason's home is on approximately how many acres?

(A)   Mason's house sits on about 1 acre of land.

(B)   Mason's house sits on about 6 acres of land.

(C)   Mason's house sits on about 10 acres of land.

(D)   Mason's house sits on about 12 acres of land.

(13)   Alex has 6 crayons, Alice has 13 crayons, Scott has 26 crayons and Melvin has 14 crayons. Approximate the average number of crayons the friends have.

(A)   59 crayons

(B)   13 crayons

(C)   15 crayons

(D)   46 crayons

(14)   Which sentence correctly states how many days are in a year?

(A)   There are 362 days in a year.

(B)   There are 365 days in a year.

(C)   There are 375 days in a year.

(D)   There are 370 days in a year.

(15)   If you are building a shed and there are a total of 36 pieces of material to build the 4 sides, what is the average number of pieces that make each side?

(A)   There are 9 pieces per side on average.

(B)   There are 8 pieces per side on average.

(C)   There are 12 pieces per side on average.

(D)   There are 36 pieces per side on average.

(16)   Finding the product of two and five means?

(A)   Addition

(B)   Subtraction

(C)   Multiplication

(D)   Division

(17)   If Anna is three times as old as Devin, what does that mean?

(A)   Anna is older than Devin.

(B)   Devin is older than Anna.

(C)   Anna and Devin are three years apart.

(D)   Devin is Anna's age multiplied by three.

(18)   What digit is in the thousandths place in the number 126,258.106?

(A)   Zero is in the thousandths place.

(B)   Six is in the thousandths place.

(C)   Two is in the thousandths place.

(D)   Five is in the thousandths place.

(19)   In the fraction $16\frac{5}{8}$ the number 16 is what part of the fraction?

(A)   Mixed number

(B)   Whole number

(C)   Numerator

(D)   Denominator

(20)   The fraction $\frac{3}{4}$ is what in decimal form?

(A)   0.75

(B)   0.25

(C)   0.50

(D)   0.30

(21)   The kangaroo can jump 12 feet into the air, the rabbit can jump 12 inches into the air, the dog can jump 36 inches and the frog can jump 4 feet in the air. Which animal can jump higher?

(A)   The frog can jump higher than the other animals.

(B)   The rabbit can jump higher than the other animals.

(C)   The kangaroo can jump higher than the other animals.

(D)   The dog can jump higher than the other animals.

(22)   Beatrice makes bracelets to sell in her jewelry store. Each bracelet gets 16 spacer beads and 8 decorative beads. If Beatrice makes 40 bracelets for the coming month, roughly how many beads will she need altogether?

(A)   Beatrice will need roughly 640 beads to make all 40 bracelets.

(B)   Beatrice will need roughly 960 beads to make all 40 bracelets.

(C)   Beatrice will need roughly 24 beads to make all 40 bracelets.

(D)   Beatrice will need roughly 320 beads to make all 40 bracelets.

(23)   Hanna wants to take a hike around the state park. The trail is 15 miles long and Hanna walks about 3.5 miles an hour. Roughly how long will it take Hanna to walk the whole trail?

(A)   It will take Hanna roughly 3 and a half hours.

(B)   It will take Hanna roughly 4 and a half hours.

(C)   It will take Hanna roughly 5 and a half hours.

(D)   It will take Hanna roughly 2 and a half hours.

(24)   What is the GCF of 123, 369, 987 and 741?

(A)   The GCF of 123, 369, 987 and 741 is 9.

(B)   The GCF of 123, 369, 987 and 741 is 30.

(C)   The GCF of 123, 369, 987 and 741 is 3.

(D)   The GCF of 123, 369, 987 and 741 is 15

(25)   What is the LCM of 2, 4, 6, 8, 10 and 12?

(A)   The LCM of 2, 4, 6, 8, 10 and 12 is 2.

(B)   The LCM of 2, 4, 6, 8, 10 and 12 is 12.

(C)   The LCM of 2, 4, 6, 8, 10 and 12 is 120.

(D)   The LCM of 2, 4, 6, 8, 10 and 12 is 10.

(26)   What are the lowest (prime) factors of 96 in lowest terms?

(A)   The lowest factors of 96 are 3 and 2.

(B)   The lowest factors of 96 are 6 and 3.

(C)   The lowest factors of 96 are 9 and 12.

(D)   The lowest factors of 96 are 12 and 6.

(27)   Which of the following numbers is a prime number?

(A)   96

(B)   97

(C)   98

(D)   99

(28)   Keisha can run 6 miles in 3 hours at a constant speed. How many miles does Keisha run in one hour?

(A)   Keisha runs 4 miles in an hour.

(B)   Keisha runs 3 miles in an hour.

(C)   Keisha runs 2 miles in an hour.

(D)   Keisha runs 1 mile in an hour.

(29)   Which of the following numbers is a multiple of 16?

(A)   106

(B)   110

(C)   160

(D)   210

(30)   Which of the following numbers is a multiple of 2?

(A)   21

(B)   34

(C)   53

(D)   61

(31)   What is the LCD of $\frac{12}{24}, \frac{36}{64}, \frac{84}{168}$?

(A)   The LCD for this set of fractions is 16.

(B)   The LCD for this set of fractions is 192.

(C)   The LCD for this set of fractions is 193.

(D)   The LCD for this set of fractions is 192.

(32)   Oliver takes his dog Dig to the dog park four days a week. The days Dig doesn't go to the park make up roughly what percentage of the week?

(A)   Dig stays home from the park 30% of the week.

(B)   Dig stays home from the park 40% of the week.

(C)   Dig stays home from the park 50% of the week.

(D)   Dig stays home from the park 60% of the week.

(33)   Sam took out a loan to buy his truck. If the loan was for $34,000 and he has an annual interest rate of 5%, how much will Sam owe on his truck altogether after one year?

(A)   Sam will owe $34,000 in total.

(B)   Sam will owe $33,500 in total.

(C)   Sam will owe $35,700 in total.

(D)   Sam will owe $37,400 in total.

(34)   If there are more green crayons than red, half as many blue crayons as green crayons, more blue crayons than purple and the same number of orange crayons as green, the greatest number of crayons are what colors?

(A)   Red and yellow

(B)   Blue and orange

(C)   Orange and green

(D)   Purple and blue

(35)   Emma is weighing in at the gym. What unit of measure will her weight be measured in?

(A)   Grams

(B)   Ounces

(C)   Pounds

(D)   Yards

(36)   If $(a + b) = (b + a)$ then $(x + y)$ must equal?

(A) $(y + x)$

(B) $(ay + bx)$

(C) $(ab + ba + xy + yx)$

(D) $(x + y + z)$

(37)   Bob's Gas and Go sold $365.29 worth of gas on Monday, $543.21 on Tuesday, $146.31 on Wednesday, $221.48 on Thursday and $617.29 on Friday. What day did Bob's sell the most gas?

(A)   Bob's Gas and Go sold the most gas on Tuesday.

(B)   Bob's Gas and Go sold the most gas on Friday.

(C)   Bob's Gas and Go sold the most gas on Wednesday.

(D)   Bob's Gas and Go sold the most gas on Monday.

(38)   If the United States imports 1/4 of items from Europe and 2/4 of items from China and the rest are made in the United States, what proportion of items are made in the United States?

(A)   1/8

(B)   1/4

(C)   1/2

(D)   3/4

Test 2: Reading Comprehension

Directions: Read each passage that follows carefully. Think about the main points, the tone and feel of the passage, the information presented and anything that you feel the passage might be implying. When you are through reading each passage, carefully read each question and the corresponding answers. Using the information you gained from the passage, choose the correct answer.

Test 2 Passage 1 & Questions:

1.   Theodor Seuss Geisel was born in Springfield, Massachusetts, on March 2, 1904.
2.   His parents were Theodor Geisel & Henrietta (Seuss) Geisel.
3.   He had one sister who was often called "Marnie"
4.   but whose given name was Margaretha Christine.
5.   His grandparents were immigrants who came to the United States from Germany.
6.   Theodor attended Dartmouth and graduated from there in June 1925.
7.   During his time there he adopted the pseudonym "Seuss,"
8.   which he used for his publications in the school's humor magazine.
9.   Following Dartmouth, he attended Lincoln College at Oxford.
10.   In 1927, Theodor changed his pseudonym to Dr. Seuss,
11.   which he continued to use throughout the rest of his life.
12.   He also used the less common pseudonym Ted LeSige,
13.   which he used for his books that were illustrated by others.
14.   While at Lincoln College, Theodor met Helen Palmer who became his wife in 1927.
15.   After some 27 rejections, Theodor was ready to give up on his writing.
16.   As luck would have it, he ran into a former classmate
17.   who was in charge of the children's division of a publishing company.
18.   He signed Theodor immediately.
19.   In 1937, *And to Think it Happened on Mulberry Street*
20.   became the first Dr. Seuss book to be published.
21.   In 1948, Theodor and Helen moved to California.
22.   In 1957, Theodor published *The Grinch Who Stole Christmas*.
23.   Theodor related to his grumpy character so much
24.   that he had a license plate that read 'Grinch' on the Buick he drove.
25.   "The Grinch Who Stole Christmas" became a TV special in 1966.
26.   The TV special was something he did together with an army buddy.
27.   In 1957, *The Cat in the Hat* was published.
28.   Like the character in his book, Theodor loved hats and had a collection of over 100 crazy hats.
29.   Dr. Seuss came out with a Beginner Book series in 1958.
30.   The series started as a challenge by an education director
31.   to write a book kids wouldn't want to stop reading,
32.   and it had to contain words from a specific list of 348 total word choices,
33.   which Dr. Seuss did, using only 236.
34.   The series was launched with *The Cat and the Hat Comes Back*, along with four other books.

35. He later published another well-known title, *Green Eggs & Ham,* in 1960.
36. He released many books in his lifetime.
37. Theodor died in 1991 and after his death his manuscripts and illustrations
38. were donated to the University of California in San Diego.
39. The college renamed the library in 1995 after him.

Directions: Using the passage above, answer each of the five questions that follow. Refer back to the passage to confirm your answer choices and refresh the details of your memory. The answers to all of the questions will either be in the passage or will require your opinion or point of view, so there is no outside information you need to know.

(1)   What name is Theodor Geisel most famously known by?

(A)   Theodor Geisel is most famous for being known as Dr. Seuss.

(B)   Theodor Geisel is most famous for being known as Ted LeSieg.

(C)   Theodor Geisel is most famous for being known as Theodor Geisel.

(D)   None of the above.

(2)   What genre of books did Dr. Seuss write?

(A)   Dr. Seuss wrote books for adults.

(B)   Dr. Seuss wrote books for young adults.

(C)   Dr. Seuss wrote books for children.

(D)   Dr. Seuss wrote books for elderly adults.

(3)   What type of car did Theodor drive?

(A)   Theodor drove a Ford.

(B)   Theodor drove a Buick.

(C)   Theodor drove a Chevrolet.

(D)   Theodor drove a Lincoln.

(4)   What made Dr. Seuss create the Beginner Book series?

(A)   The Dr. Seuss Beginner Book series was started out of boredom.

(B)   The Dr. Seuss Beginner Book series was started because of a challenge.

(C)   The Dr. Seuss Beginner Book series was started because of his love for writing.

(D)   The Dr. Seuss Beginner Book series was started by his wife.

(5)   Which book became a TV special?

(A)   The book *The Cat in the Hat* became a TV special.

(B)   The book *Green Eggs and Ham* became a TV special.

(C)   The book *The Cat and the Hat Comes Back* became a TV special.

(D)   The book *The Grinch who Stole Christmas* became a TV special.

Test 2 Passage 2 & Questions:

1.   More than two-thirds of homes in America have video games of one form or another.

2.   Today the video game world is a conglomerate worth over 100 billion dollars,

3.   spread over a vast array of gaming systems.

4.   Some of those systems include PCs, the Xbox, the PS4, the Wii and handheld games.

5.   Though there were some basic video games created in the '50s,

6.   the systems we see now were born from an invention by Steven Russell in 1962.

7.   Russell attended MIT and created the first video game that could be played on multiple

8.   computer installations.

9.   This was cutting-edge technology for its time,

10.   comprised of a Programmed Data Processor-1 or PDP-1.

11.   The PDP-1 was a computer that was almost exclusively found in universities at the time.

12.   Atari released the arcade game Pong in 1972, the first of its kind.

13.   Atari went on to release a household Pong game in 1975

14.   and a computer-based Atari in 1977.

15.   The 1970s and 1980s were a major time of growth for the video-game world.

16.   Games including Pac-Man and Donkey Kong were released and hugely successful.

17.   Microsoft also developed and released its first flight simulator game.

18.   In 1983 the video-game world experienced a major fall, though.

19.   Video games were being released at a high rate, with a lot of advertising and bad quality.

20.   Computer-based video games were becoming more popular than the gaming console,

21.   and the U.S. market was overflowing with far too many systems.

22.   This all led to a major fall in the industry.

23.   In 1985, Nintendo worked to create better games with better graphics.

24.   They later released big-ticket games like Super Mario Brothers and The Legend of Zelda.

25.   These games are still hugely popular and have become franchises of their own today,

26.   though much improved from their original formats.

27.   Video games have grown over the decades to the in-depth creations we have now.

28.   3D graphics and the internet allow for multiplayer gaming, just to name a few of those.

29. Technology, computers, gaming systems and graphics are improving every day.
30. The future holds so many possibilities for the world of gaming.
31. One day we might even be able to step into our gaming worlds and experience them first-hand.

Directions: Using the passage above, answer each of the five questions that follow. Refer back to the passage to confirm your answer choices and refresh the details of your memory. The answers to all of the questions will either be in the passage or require your opinion or point of view, so there is no outside information you need to know.

(1)   How much is the video game industry worth today?

(A)   The video game industry is worth a hundred million dollars.

(B)   The video game industry is worth a hundred thousand dollars.

(C)   The video game industry is worth a hundred billion dollars.

(D)   The video game industry is worth a hundred trillion dollars.

(2)   In what decade was the most basic video game created?

(A)   The most basic video game was created in the '80s.

(B)   The most basic video game was created in the '90s.

(C)   The most basic video game was created in the '60s.

(D)   The most basic video game was created in the '50s.

(3)   Who created the games Super Mario Brothers and The Legend of Zelda?

(A)   Atari

(B)   Nintendo

(C)   MIT

(D)   Microsoft

(4)   What company developed the first flight simulator?

(A)   Microsoft

(B)   Atari

(C)   Sega

(D)   Nintendo

(5)   Why did the United States experience a "crash" in the video game industry?

(A)   Gaming consoles were too expensive and they were hard to come by.

(B)   Video games were unpopular at the time.

(C)   The market was flooded with them and they were produced poorly.

(D)   Outdoor sports were more popular, so video game sales fell.

Test 2 Passage 3 & Questions:

1.   Princess Sophie of Alhalt-Zerbst was born on May 2, 1729. She would later be known as

2.   Catherine the Great and would be Russia's longest-reigning female ruler.

3.   She married Peter III of Russia in 1745

4.   He became emperor of Russia on January 5, 1762.

5.   With his ascension, Catherine became empress consort of Russia.

6.   She held the title of empress consort until she staged a coup and overthrew her husband's rule on July 9, 1762,

7.   doing so because she felt he was a weak man who was taking poor care of Russia.

8.   She had her official coronation on September 22, 1762.

9.   She ruled over Russia until her death on November 17, 1796.

10.   During her time as empress, she made massive improvements to Russia as a whole.

11.   She expanded Russia by 200,000 miles.

12.   She also forged a great trading alliance with Great Britain.

13.   The alliance was for goods and services, not for any military support, as many alliances are.

14.   Catherine the Great supported Western education and culture.

15.   She brought aspects of it into Russia's culture and development,

16.   even going so far as to encourage and foster the education of Russian children.

17.   Religion became less important during her reign.

18.   She changed the way nobles and servants operated and how they treated one another.

19.   One of Catherine the Great's greatest medical achievements was to bring vaccines to Russia

20.   at a time when many people were skeptical or even outright afraid of medical advances.

21.   She chose to lead by example and had herself vaccinated for smallpox on October 12, 1768.

22.   While she developed a light case of smallpox, she was fully recovered by the end of the month.

23.   Later she also had her children vaccinated and by the early 1780s,

24.   her actions had prompted more than two million Russians to also be vaccinated.

25.   Catherine the Great's reign ended with her death on November 17, 1796.

26.   Her son, Paul I of Russia, ascended the throne upon her death.

27.   Catherine the Great's reign was coined the Catherinian Era

28.   and is said to have marked the Golden Age of Russia.

29.   Her time as empress of Russia made the country better

30.   economically, agriculturally, medically, intellectually and culturally.

Directions: Using the passage above, answer each of the five questions that follow. Refer back to the passage to confirm your answer choices and refresh the details of your memory. The answers to all of the questions will either be in the passage or will require your opinion or point of view, so there is no outside information you need to know.

(1)   How did Catherine the Great become empress of Russia?

(A)   Catherine the Great became empress of Russia when she married its emperor.

(B)   Catherine the Great became empress of Russia when her father died and she became empress.

(C)   Catherine the Great became empress of Russia when she stole the crown from her weak husband.

(D)   She was never empress; she was only the empress consort of Russia.

(2)   When did Catherine become empress of Russia?

(A)   Catherine the Great became empress of Russia on May 2, 1729.

(B)   Catherine the Great became empress of Russia on January 5, 1762.

(C)   Catherine the Great became empress of Russia on July 9, 1762.

(D)   Catherine the Great became empress of Russia on November 17, 1796.

(3)   What great medical advance came to Russia during Catherine's reign?

(A)   Catherine the Great brought surgery to Russia during her reign.

(B)   Catherine the Great brought vaccines to Russia during her reign.

(C)   Catherine the Great brought herbal medicine to Russia during her reign.

(D)   None of the above.

(4)   Who was Catherine's successor?

(A)   Catherine the Great was succeeded by her son, Paul I, upon her death.

(B)   Catherine the Great was succeeded by her son, Peter III, upon her death.

(C)   Catherine the Great was succeeded by her son, Corn Wallace, upon her death.

(D)   Catherine the Great was succeeded by her son, the British king, upon her death.

(5)   What was rare about her alliance with Great Britain?

(A)   Catherine the Great made an alliance without marriage and without securing borders.

(B)   Catherine the Great made an alliance without a marriage alliance.

(C)   Catherine the Great made an alliance without marriage and without military support.

(D)   None of the above.

Test 2 Passage 4 & Questions:

1.   If you visit the National Museum of African American History and Culture,
2.   you might just meet Pepper.
3.   No, Pepper isn't an animal or a person.
4.   Pepper is a humanoid robot who is four-foot tall.
5.   Pepper was created by Softbank Robotics.
6.   Pepper is the first of its kind and the Smithsonian Institute is the very first educational
7.   research museum to experiment with the use of its technology.
8.   There is a tablet on Pepper's chest that allows words, images and videos to be viewed.
9.   Pepper can pose for selfies, dance and play games.
10.   Pepper can tell stories and answer your questions.
11.   Pepper's answers are all prerecorded and work on a standard response system.

Directions: Using the passage above, answer each of the five questions that follow. Refer back to the passage to confirm your answer choices and refresh the details of your memory. The answers to all of the questions will either be in the passage or will require your opinion or point of view, so there is no outside information you need to know.

(1)   What is Pepper?

(A)   Pepper is a therapy dog.

(B)   Pepper is a humanoid robot.

(C)   Pepper is a security guard.

(D)   Pepper is a museum technology.

(2)   Who made Pepper?

(A)   Pepper was made by the Smithsonian.

(B)   Pepper was made by the Museum of Natural History.

(C)   Pepper was made by Softbank Robotics.

(D)   Pepper was made by the Renwick Gallery.

(3)   How does Pepper respond to questions?

(A)   Pepper responds to questions with prerecorded answers.

(B)   Pepper answers each question with answers.

(C)   Pepper can't talk.

(D)   Pepper responds with answers on his tablet.

(4)   Where can you see Pepper right now?

(A)   You can meet Pepper at the National American History Museum.

(B)   You can meet Pepper at the National Museum of African American History and Culture.

(C)   You can meet Pepper at the American Indian Museum Heye Center.

(D)   None of the above.

(5)   What fun things can Pepper do with you?

(A)   Pepper can dance and play games.

(B)   Pepper can play games and watch TV.

(C)   Pepper can sing songs and dance.

(D)   Pepper can draw and race cars.

Test 2 Passage 5 & Questions:

1.   Oscoda, Michigan, is located on the shores of Lake Huron in Northern Michigan.
2.   The town is now a seasonal tourist town and generates the majority of its revenue that way.
3.   The town is known as the home of Paul Bunyan.
4.   It got that reputation because the first story of Paul Bunyan was printed in its local newspaper.
5.   The town was originally the home of many lumberjacks because of its rich, dense forests.
6.   Later it became the home of an Air Force base.
7.   The Air Force brought a great deal of revenue to the area
8.   as well as increasing the local population.
9.   When the Air Force base was closed, it impacted the town heavily.
10.   With the military gone and the days of the lumberjacks long behind it,
11.   Oscoda now relies on its famous white sand beaches,
12.   air museum, lakes, forests, historical landmarks, nearby lighthouses
13.   and historic neighboring cities to draw in the tourists and carry the town
14.   through from season to season.
15.   The locals enjoy the beautiful natural forests,
16.   crystal-clear lakes,
17.   white sand beaches,
18.   charming local pubs,
19.   and year-round natural beauty.
20.   So, if you don't call Oscoda your home,
21.   consider making it a vacation spot
22.   and enjoy the beauty it has to offer.

Directions Using the passage above, answer each of the five questions that follow. Refer back to the passage to confirm your answer choices and refresh the details of your memory. The answers to all of the questions will either be in the passage or will require your opinion or point of view, so there is no outside information you need to know.

(1)   Where is Oscoda located?

(A)   Oscoda is located in Northern Michigan.

(B)   Oscoda is located on Lake Superior.

(C)   Oscoda is located on an Air Force base.

(D)   None of the above.

(2)   What is Oscoda's source of revenue today?

(A)   Oscoda earns the majority of its revenue from lumber.

(B)   Oscoda earns the majority of its revenue from fishing.

(C)   Oscoda earns the majority of its revenue from tourists.

(D)   Oscoda earns the majority of its revenue from pubs.

(3)   What famous lumberjack is associated with Oscoda?

(A)   Babe the Blue Ox

(B)   Paul Bunyan

(C)   Babe Ruth

(D)   Charles Lindbergh

(4)   If a man is called a lumberjack, what do you think a female lumberjack is called?

(A)   There is no such thing; women aren't lumberjacks.

(B)   A female lumberjack is referred to as a lumber jill.

(C)   A female lumberjack is just called a lumberjack.

(D)   None of the above.

(5)   What kinds of beaches is Oscoda known for?

(A)   Oscoda is known for its white sand beaches.

(B)   Oscoda is known for its crystal-clear waters.

(C)   Oscoda is known for its natural beauty.

(D)   None of the above.

Test 2 Mathematics Achievement

Directions: In this Mathematics Achievement practice test you will find a variety of mathematical questions that test your math skills as well as the information you have learned. The questions may include addition, subtraction, multiplication and division, as well as square roots, geometry, measurements, probability and overall problem-solving.

Read each question carefully. Then read each of the multiple-choice questions that follow. Choose the answer that correctly solves each question, word problem or equation. On your official exam, you will be allowed to use the space in your workbook or margins to solve the equations. With that in mind, you may use scratch paper to work the equations in this study guide.

(1)   Mr. Evens' class has 3 kids with blond hair, 4 kids with brown hair, 1 with red hair and 2 with black. What percentage of kids have blond hair?

(A)   30% of the kids in Mr. Evens' class have blond hair.

(B)   50% of the kids in Mr. Evens' class have blond hair.

(C)   75% of the kids in Mr. Evens' class have blond hair.

(D)   10% of the kids in Mr. Evens' class have blond hair.

(2)   What is the GCF of 3, 9 and 22?

(A)   The GCF of 3, 9 and 22 is 7.

(B)   The GCF of 3, 9 and 22 is 5.

(C)   The GCF of 3, 9 and 22 is 3.

(D)   The GCF of 3, 9 and 22 is 1.

(3)   Angela runs five miles on Monday, eight miles on Wednesday, seven miles on Friday and four miles on the other four days of the week. How many miles does Angel run in a week?

(A)   Every week, Angela runs 36 miles.

(B)   Every week, Angela runs 24 miles.

(C)   Every week, Angela runs 38 mils.

(D)   Every week, Angela runs 26 miles.

(4)   Mark lives on Pine Street and works on Maple Drive. He takes his dog Murphy to the park on Sycamore and gets his groceries at the market on Birch every day before going home. Mark and Murphy walk the four miles from his house on Pine to his office on Maple. The distance from Pine to Maple and Sycamore to Birch is the same. The distance from Maple to Sycamore and the distance from Birch to Pine is the same. If the total distance of Mark's walk is 28 miles, what is the distance between Maple and Sycamore and between Birch and Pine?

(A)   The distance is 10 miles.

(B)   The distance is 20 miles.

(C)   The distance is 8 miles.

(D)   The distance is 12 miles.

(5)   Which of the following answers correctly shows the square root of forty-four?

(A) $\sqrt{40}$

(B) $\sqrt[3]{44}$

(C) $\frac{\pi}{2}$

(D) $\sqrt{44}$

(6)   16 is the square root of which number?

(A)   16 is the square root of 256.

(B)   16 is the square root of 265.

(C)   16 is the square root of 216.

(D)   16 is the square root of 266.

(7)   What is the diameter of the circle?

(A)   The diameter of the circle is 15 inches.

(B)   The diameter of the circle is 30 inches.

(C)   The diameter of the circle is 60 inches.

(D)   The diameter of the circle is 35 inches.

(8)   What is the square root of 16?

(A)   The square root of 16 is 2.

(B)   The square root of 16 is 3.

(C)   The square root of 16 is 4.

(D)   The square root of 16 is 6.

(9)   One hundred twenty-five million, two hundred fifty-six thousand, and two-hundredths is correctly expressed as a numerical value in which answer?

(A)   125,256,002

(B)   125,256,000.02

(C)   125,000256.02

(D)   1,250,256.20

(10)   What two ways can you write the number 1,500?

(A)   Fifteen hundred or one thousand five hundred

(B)   Five hundred thousand or fifteen thousand

(C)   Fifteen thousand or fifteen hundred

(D)   Fifteen hundred thousand or five hundred thousand

(11)   Five hundred and twenty-five thousandths is correctly expressed in which of the following numerical values?

(A)   500.025

(B)   525.00

(C)   0.525

(D)   5.25

(12) Which answer correctly expresses one and five-eighths?

(A) $\frac{1}{58}$

(B) $\frac{5}{8}$

(C) $1\frac{5}{8}$

(D) $8\frac{1}{5}$

(13) What is the place value of the 9 in 154,522,784.29 ?

(A) thousands

(B) hundredths

(C) thousandths

(D) tens

(14) The cake mix is 60% flour and 8% wet ingredients. What percentage makes up the rest of the batter?

(A) 32%

(B) 24%

(C) 43%

(D) 18%

(15) If you have a six-sided dice numbered one through six, what is the probability of rolling a six?

(A) 1 in 6

(B) 2 in 4

(C) 3 in 5

(D) 1 in 3

(16) The dogs at the animal shelter get two cups of food twice a day. A bag of dog food has 184 one-cup servings. If there are seven dogs at the shelter, how many bags of dog food does the shelter need to buy to feed all seven dogs for the first week?

(A) The shelter needs to buy 6 bags of dog food for the first week.

(B) The shelter needs to buy 4 bags of dog food for the first week.

(C) The shelter needs to buy 2 bags of dog food for the first week.

(D) The shelter needs to buy 8 bags of dog food for the first week.

(17) Oreo the cow weighs 506 pounds, Marvin the orangutan weighs 96 pounds and Lilly the hippo weighs 957 pounds. How much would their combined weight be and could all three animals ride on a truck that can carry 1 ton?

(A) No, they would weigh 1,559 pounds and be too heavy for a 1-ton truck.

(B) Yes, they would weigh 1,559 pounds and would be light enough to ride in the truck.

(C) No, they would weigh more than 1 ton and would be too heavy for the truck.

(D) None of the above.

(18) Helen is four foot three inches, Megan is five foot six inches, Tasha is five foot two inches and Danielle is four foot nine inches. What is the average height of the girls, rounded to the nearest inch?

(A) The average height of the girls is 5 feet 4 inches.

(B) The average height of the girls is 5 feet 2 inches.

(C) The average height of the girls is 4 feet 11 inches.

(D) The average height of the girls is 4 feet 9 inches.

(19) Using $a = 12$, $c = 37$ and $b = 49$, solve the equation: $(a + b) \times (b - c) = $ ____?

(A) 237

(B) 730

(C) 327

(D) 732

173

(20) Using $a = 12$, solve the equation for c: $4 + 9 + 6 - a = c$

(A) 19

(B) 7

(C) 32

(D) 2

(21) Sam is sending a package to his brother in Florida. The box cost $5.46, the tape cost $1.50, the packing peanuts were 79 cents and the postage was $45 with the shipping insurance. If the package is taxed at 9%, what will Sam's total be for sending the package?

(A) Sam's package will cost him $54.49 after taxes.

(B) Sam's package will cost him $62.98 after taxes.

(C) Sam's package will cost him $49.95 after taxes.

(D) Sam's package will cost him $57.50 after taxes.

(22) Round the number 789,654 to the nearest hundred.

(A) 789,700

(B) 789,650

(C) 790,000

(D) 789,640

(23) What is the circumference of the circle if the area is 81π?

(A) 9π

(B) 36π

(C) 18π

(D) 45π

(24)   What is the place value of the 9 in the number 874,563,912?

(A)   Hundreds

(B)   Hundredths

(C)   Ten thousandth

(D)   Millionth

(25)   Tristan is building a rectangle deck off the back of his house. If the deck is 15 feet wide by 36 feet long, what is the area of the deck?

(A)   The area of Tristan's deck is 540 square feet.

(B)   The area of Tristan's deck is 1836 square feet.

(C)   The area of Tristan's deck is 945 square feet.

(D)   The area of Tristan's deck is 51 square feet.

(26)   Jason is building a fishing cabin on the lake. The cabin will be 168 feet wide by 200 feet long. What is the area of Jason's cabin?

(A)   The area of Jason's fishing cabin is 500 square feet.

(B)   The area of Jason's fishing cabin is 33,600 square feet.

(C)   The area of Jason's fishing cabin is 368 square feet.

(D)   The area of Jason's fishing cabin is 34,620 square feet.

(27)   Anna and her mother are selling pies at the county fair this weekend. They are selling their pies for $7.25 each. How many pies did Anna sell if she made $891.75?

(A)   Anna sold 112 pies.

(B)   Anna sold 168 pies.

(C)   Anna sold 138 pies.

(D)   Anna sold 123 pies.

(28)   Solve for *a* and round to the nearest whole number. $125 \div 5 + 47.25 + 14.386 = a$.

(A)   86.636

(B)   87

(C)   85

(D)   86.64

(29)   Put the following fractions in order from least to greatest: 1/2, 1/4, 1/3.

(A)   1/3, 1/4, 1/2

(B)   1/4, 1/3, 1/2

(C)   1/2, 1/3, 1/4

(D)   1/2, 1/4, 1/3

(30)   What place value is the 7, in the number 7,000?

(A)   Thousands

(B)   Millions

(C)   Thousandths

(D)   Hundredths

Test 2 Essay Question

Unlike the other portions of your practice test, there is no right or wrong answer for your essay, so this portion of your practice test will not have an answer section.

Essay Topic

If you were asked to tell someone about your life, what are the most important things you would want someone to know, and why do you think it's important that they know them?

Test 2 Answers – Verbal Reasoning

In this Practice Test Answer Key, you will find the correct answer for each of the questions on Practice Test 2. The correct answer will be followed by an explanation to clarify why that answer is correct.

Test 2 Synonyms – Answers

(1)   The correct answer is: **B) withdraw – to leave physically or mentally, give up or retreat.**

RETIRE – to stop working, go to bed or withdraw. The answer that has the closest meaning to RETIRE is **withdraw.**

(2)   The correct answer is: **C) reclaim – to restore, take back or rescue.**

SALVAGE – to save, rescue, conserve or restore. The answer that has the closest meaning to SALVAGE is **reclaim.**

(3)   The correct answer is: **A) frugal – prudent, sparing or stingy.**

THRIFTY – financially careful. The answer that has the closest meaning to THRIFTY is **frugal.**

(4)   The correct answer is: **D) undisputed – certain, undoubted or unquestionable.**

UNANIMOUS – in complete agreement. The answer that has the closest meaning to UNANIMOUS is **undisputed.**

(5)   The correct answer is: **D) obvious – easily noticed.**

VISIBLE – in sight, detectable or obvious. The answer that has the closest meaning to VISIBLE is **obvious.**

(6)   The correct answer is: **A) extract – to take out, remove or haul.**

WITHDRAW – to remove, retreat or pull out. The answer that has the closest meaning to WITHDRAW is **extract.**

(7)   The correct answer is: **C) belligerent – quarrelsome, confrontational or aggressive.**

AGGRESSIVE – attacking, violent or destructive. The answer that has the closest meaning to AGGRESSIVE is **belligerent.**

(8)   The correct answer is: **B) unruly – disorderly, rowdy or boisterous.**

BOISTEROUS – noisy, rowdy or overexcited. The answer that has the closest meaning to BOISTEROUS is **unruly.**

(9)   The correct answer is: **D) confront – face up to, meet head-on or deal with**.

CHALLENGE – to defy, dispute or dare. The answer that has the closest meaning to CHALLENGE is **confront.**

(10)   The correct answer is: **D) exhaust – meaning to tire out or use up.**

DEPLETE – empty, drain, remove from the source or use up. The answer that has the closest meaning to DEPLETE is **exhaust.**

(11)   The correct answer is: **A) infuriate – to enrage, madden, annoy or irritate.**

EXASPERATE – to anger, worsen or frustrate. The answer that has the closest meaning to EXASPERATE is **infuriate.**

(12)   The correct answer is: **C) mingle – to blend, merge or unite.**

FUSE – to combine or blend. The answer that has the closest meaning to FUSE is **mingle.**

(13)   The correct answer is: **B) gluttonous – to overstuff, overeat or be greedy.**

GORGE – to overeat, stuff yourself or a chasm. The answer that has the closest meaning to GORGE is **gluttonous.**

(14)   The correct answer is: **D) locale – backdrop, surroundings or environment.**

HABITAT – a home, environment or surroundings. The answer that has the closest meaning to HABITAT is **locale.**

(15)   The correct answer is: **C) illumine – light or light up.**

ILLUMINATE – light up, enlighten or make clear. The answer that is closest in meaning to ILLUMINATE is **illumine.**

(16)   The correct answer is: **A) talent – forte, gift or aptitude.**

KNACK – ability, skill or gift. The answer that has the closest meaning to KNACK is **talent.**

(17)   The correct answer is: **B) deluxe – superior, exclusive or sumptuous.**

LUXURIOUS – comfortable, deluxe or lavish. The answer that has the closest meaning to LUXURIOUS is **deluxe.**

Test 2 Sentence Completion – Answers

(1)   The correct answer is: **B) unrealistic – not reasonable or unlikely.**

Completing 400 orders by the end of the day was completely **unrealistic**.

(2)   The correct answer is: **C) solar – requiring the sun or sunlight.**

The rooftops of the houses were covered in **solar** panels.

(3)   The correct answer is: **C) would not be soothed – would not be comforted or calmed.**

The baby was crying frantically and **would not be soothed.**

(4)   The correct answer is: **D) massive – extremely large or gigantic.**

The Ferris wheel was **massive** and overshadowed all of the other carnival rides.

(5)   The correct answer is: **A) navigate – to steer or find the way.**

The GPS was supposed to help my father to **navigate** to our destination, but he didn't use it.

(6)   The correct answer is: **B) obstacles – impediments or blockages.**

The course had a lot of **obstacles** that we had to evade in order to reach the finish line.

(7)   The correct answer is: **C) passage – channel, route or opening.**

There was a secret **passage** behind the tapestry in the hall.

(8)   The correct answer is: **D) abundance – large amount, plenty.**

There was an **abundance** of food after the harvest, so we shared the bounty.

(9)   The correct answer is: **A) beverages – drinks.**

Coke, lemonade, coffee, tea and water are the **beverages** offered at the restaurant.

(10)   The correct answer is: **B) companion – friend, buddy.**

My dad got Charlie, a 75-pound mastiff, as a **companion** so he wouldn't be alone anymore.

(11)   The correct answer is: **B) duplicated – To make a copy, spare or replica.**

I wanted to have a clone, so I **duplicated** myself to get one.

(12)   The correct answer is: **C) my boss told me I had done an inferior job.**

I was feeling diminished after **my boss told me I had done an inferior job.**

Explanation: Answers A, B and D all use words that mean the person did well or performed their duties at or above the required standard. Answer C is the only option that shows dissatisfaction and therefore would make the individual feel small.

(13)   The correct answer is: **D) inedible – unable to be eaten.**

The fruit in the basket were in fact wax and completely **inedible**.

(14)   The correct answer is: **A) fused – joined or melded.**

The chocolate had melted together and the chocolate-covered strawberries were **fused** together.

(15) The correct answer is: **B) glare – to look angry or fierce, to glower.**

The sun through my office window left a horrible **glare** on my computer screen.

(16) The correct answer is: **C) history – a past occurrence or series of events.**

If we do not remember our **history,** we are doomed to repeat it.

(17) The correct answer is: **C) There it is!**

As we approached the pier, Sarah pointed to her favorite ride and squealed, **"There it is!"**

Explanation: "Their" is used to reference a person. "They're" is the contraction of they and are. "There" is used to reference a place in time or the location of something.

Test 2 Answers – Quantitative Reasoning

(1)   The correct answer is: **B) number of horses x (2(g) +1(o))**

(2)   The correct answer is: **A) $84 ÷ 2 = t$**

(3)   The correct answer is: **D) π**

(4)   The correct answer is: **D) Justin had his best sales in 2017 and 2019.**

EXPLANATION: Based on the chart, Justin sold over 200 supplies in 2019, almost 175 in 2017, fewer than 150 supplies in 2018 and had 100 sales in 2016. Therefore, he sold the most supplies in 2017 and 2019.

(5)   The correct answer is: **B) The paddock will be in the shape of a rectangle.**

(6)   The correct answer is: **B) There are 5 spaces for compact cars.**

Explanation: There are 19 spaces in total. If you have 6 full size, 6 economy and 2 electric spaces, that is a total of (6 + 6 + 2) or 14 spaces that are already taken. Take the total spaces (19) and subtract the spaces already taken (14), to leave 5 spaces for compact cars.

(7)   The correct answer is: **A) There are 7 lemurs in the last enclosure.**

EXPLANATION: There are 27 lemurs in total. There are a total of 6 enclosures. There are 4 lemurs in the first 5 enclosures. Take the 5 enclosures multiplied by the 4 lemurs that are in each enclosure (5 × 4 = 20). Then take the total number of lemurs (27) and subtract the number of lemurs in the first five enclosures (20) to leave 7 lemurs in the last enclosure.

(8)   The correct answer is: **D) Miles.**

(9)   The correct answer is: **C) 25 < 45.**

(10)   The correct answer is: **D) Tons**.

EXPLANATION: A ton is a unit of measurement for incredibly large amounts of something. In this case, a whale. Semitrucks, shipping containers and other large mammals are also weighed by the ton.

(11)   The correct answer is: **B) Bushel.**

(12)   The correct answer is: **D) Mason's house sits on around 12 acres of land.**

(13)   The correct answer is: **C) 15 crayons.**

(14)   The correct answer is: **B) There are 365 days in a year.**

(15)   The correct answer is: **A) There are 9 pieces per side on average.**

EXPLANATION: There are 4 sides to the shed and a total of 36 pieces. If there are the same number of pieces to build each side you divide the number of total pieces (36) by the number of sides to be built (4) to get the average number of pieces per side, so $36 \div 4 = 9$.

(16)   The correct answer is: **C) Multiplication.**

(17)   The correct answer is: **A) Anna is older than Devin.**

(18)   The correct answer is: **B) Six is in the thousandths place.**

(19)   The correct answer is: **B) Whole number.**

(20)   The correct answer is: **A) 0.75.**

EXPLANATION: Turn 3/4 into an equivalent fraction with the denominator of 100, by multiplying the denominator and numerator by 25. The new fraction is 75/100. 75/100 is the same as 75% and 75% written as a decimal is 0.75.

(21)   The correct answer is: **C) The kangaroo can jump higher than the other animals.**

(22)   The correct answer is: **B) Beatrice will need roughly 960 beads to make all 40 bracelets.**

(23)   The correct answer is: **B) It will take Hanna roughly 4 and a half hours.**

(24)   The correct answer is: **C) The GCF of 123, 369, 987 and 741 is 3.**

(25)   The correct answer is: **C) The LCM of 2, 4, 6, 8, 10 and 12 is 120.**

(26)   The correct answer is: **A) The lowest (prime) factors of 96 are 3 and 2.**

(27)   The correct answer is: **B) 97.**

(28)   The correct answer is: **C) Keisha runs 2 miles in an hour.**

(29)   The correct answer is: **C) 160.**

(30)   The correct answer is: **B) 34.**

(31)   The correct answer is: **A) The LCD for this set of fractions is 16.**

Explanation: The LCD is the Lowest Common Denominator. The denominator is the bottom number of a fraction. In order to solve equations, you should reduce the fractions first, and then convert the denominators so they are all the same. The first fraction 12/24 reduces to 1/2. The second fraction 36/64 reduces to 9/16 and the third fraction 84/168 reduces to 1/2. The denominators are now 2, 16, and 2, which have an LCD of 16.

(32)   The correct answer is: **B) Dig stays home from the park 40% of the week.**

(33)   The correct answer is: **C) Sam will owe $35,700 in total.**

(34)   The correct answer is: **C) Orange and green**

(35)   The correct answer is: **C) Pounds.**

(36)   The correct answer is: **A) (y + x).**

(37)   The correct answer is: **B) Bob's Gas and Go sold the most gas on Friday.**

(38)   The correct answer is: **B) 1/4.**

EXPLANATION: In this problem, the United States, China and Europe make up a fraction of 4/4 or 1 whole. Since 1/4 + 2/4 = 3/4, Europe and China make up 3/4 of the items, which leaves 1/4 of the items to be made in the U.S.

Test 2 Answers – Reading Comprehension

Test 2 Passage 1 – Answers

This passage is about Theodor Geisel, more famously known as Dr. Seuss.

(1)   The correct answer is: **A) Theodor Geisel's is most famous for being known as Dr. Seuss.**
QUESTION: What name is Theodor Geisel known by?

EXPLANATION: The answer can be found in lines 7 and 10-11: "During his time there he adopted the pseudonym 'Seuss,' ... In 1927 Theodor changed his pseudonym to Dr. Seuss, which he continued to use throughout the rest of his life."

(2)   The correct answer is: **C) Dr. Seuss wrote books for children.**

QUESTION: What genre of books did Dr. Seuss write?

EXPLANATION: The answer can be found in lines 16-18: "As luck would have it, he ran into a former classmate, who was in charge of the children's division of a publishing company. He signed Theodor immediately."

(3)   The correct answer is: **B) Theodor drove a Buick.**

QUESTION: What type of car did Theodor drive?

EXPLANATION: The answer to this question can be found in line 24: "...he had a license plate that read 'Grinch' on the Buick he drove."

(4)   The correct answer is: **B) The Dr. Seuss Beginner Book series was started as a challenge.**

QUESTION: What made Dr. Seuss create the Beginner Book series?

EXPLANATION: The answer for this can be found in lines 29-31: "Dr. Seuss came out with a Beginner Book series in 1958. The series started as a challenge by an education director to write a book kids wouldn't want to stop reading."

(5)   The correct answer is: **D) The book *The Grinch Who Stole Christmas* became a TV special.**

QUESTION: Which book became a TV special?

EXPLANATION: The answer to this question can be found in lines 25-26: "*The Grinch Who Stole Christmas* became a TV special in 1966. The TV special was something he did together with an army buddy."

Test 2 Passage 2 – Answers

This passage is about the birth of the video game industry and how far it has come since its inception.

(1)   The correct answer is: **C) The video game industry is worth a hundred billion dollars.**

QUESTION: How much is the video game industry worth today?

EXPLANATION: The answer can be found in line 2: "Today the video game world is a conglomerate worth over 100 billion dollars."

(2)   The correct answer is: **D) The most basic video game was created in the '50s.**

QUESTION: In what decade was the most basic video game created?

EXPLANATION: The answer to this question can be found in line 5: "Though there were some basic video games created in the '50s."

(3)   The correct answer is: **B) Nintendo**

QUESTION: Who created games like Super Mario Brothers and The Legend of Zelda?

EXPLANATION: The answer to this question can be found in lines 23-24: "In 1985, Nintendo worked to create better games with better graphics. They later released big-ticket games like Super Mario Brothers and The Legend of Zelda."

(4)   The correct answer is: **A) Microsoft**

QUESTION: What company developed the first flight simulator?

EXPLANATION: The answer to this question can be found in line 17: "Microsoft also developed and released its first flight simulator game."

(5)   The correct answer is: **C) The market was flooded with them and they were produced poorly.**

QUESTION: Why did the United States experience a "crash" in the video game industry?

EXPLANATION: The answer can be found in lines 18-22: "In 1983, the video game world experienced a major fall, though. Video games were being released at a high rate, with a lot of advertising and bad quality. Computer-based video games were becoming more popular than the gaming console, and the U.S. market was overflowing with far too many systems. This all led to a major fall in the industry."

Test 2 Passage 3 – Answers

(1)   The correct answer is: **C) Catherine the Great became empress of Russia when she stole the crown from her weak husband.**

QUESTION: How did Catherine the Great become empress of Russia?

EXPLANATION: The answer to this question can be found in lines 6-7: "She held the title of empress consort until she staged a coup and overthrew her husband's rule on July 9, 1972, doing so because she felt he was a weak man who was taking poor care of Russia."

(2)   The correct answer is: **C) Catherine the Great became empress of Russia on July 9, 1762.**

QUESTION: When did Catherine become empress of Russia?

EXPLANATION: The answer can be found in line 6: "She held the title of empress consort until she staged a coup and overthrew her husband's rule on July 9, 1762."

(3)   The correct answer is: **B) Catherine the Great brought vaccines to Russia during her reign.**

QUESTION: What great medical advance came to Russia during Catherine's reign?

EXPLANATION: This answer can be found in line 19: "One of Catherine the Great's greatest medical achievements was to bring vaccines to Russia."

(4)   The correct answer is: **A) Catherine the Great was succeeded by her son, Paul I, upon her death.**

QUESTION: Who was Catherine's successor?

EXPLANATION: The answer to this question can be found in lines 25-26: "Catherine the Great's reign ended with her death on November 17, 1796. Her son, Paul I of Russia, ascended the throne upon her death."

(5)   The correct answer is: **C) Catherine the Great made an alliance without marriage or military support.**

QUESTION: What was rare about her alliance with Great Britain?

EXPLANATION: The answer to this question is supported in lines 12-13: "She also forged a great trading alliance with Great Britain. The alliance was for goods and services, not for any military support, as many alliances are."

Test 2 Passage 4 – Answers

This passage is about the introduction of Pepper, the humanoid robot, who is the newest addition to the Smithsonian Institute family.

(1)   The correct answer is: **B) Pepper is a humanoid robot.**

QUESTION: What is Pepper?

EXPLANATION: The answer to this question can be found in line 4: "Pepper is a humanoid robot who is four-foot tall."

(2)   The correct answer is: **C) Pepper was made by Softbank Robotics.**

QUESTION: Who made Pepper?

EXPLANATION: The answer to this question can be found in line 5: "Pepper was created by Softbank Robotics."

(3)   The correct answer is: **A) Pepper responds with prerecorded answers.**

QUESTION: How does Pepper respond to questions?

EXPLANATION: The answer to this question can be found in line 11: "Pepper's answers are all prerecorded and work on a standard response system."

(4)   The correct answer is: **B) You can meet Pepper at the National Museum of African American History and Culture.**

QUESTION: Where can you see Pepper right now?

EXPLANATION: The answer to this question can be found in lines 1-2: "If you visit the National Museum of African American History and Culture, you might just meet Pepper."

(5)   The correct answer is: **A) Pepper can dance and play games.**

QUESTION: What fun things can Pepper do with you?

EXPLANATION: The answer to this question can be found in line 9: "Pepper can pose for selfies, dance and play games."

Test 2 Passage 5 – Answers

This passage is about Oscoda, Michigan, and its history.

(1)   The correct answer is: **A) Oscoda is located in Northern Michigan.**

QUESTION: Where is Oscoda located?

EXPLANATION: The answer to this question can be found in line 1: "Oscoda, Michigan, is located on the shores of Lake Huron in Northern Michigan."

(2)   The correct answer is: **C) Oscoda earns the majority of its revenue from tourists.**

QUESTION: What is Oscoda's source of revenue today?

EXPLANATION: The answer to this question can be found in lines 11-14: "Oscoda relies on its famous white sand beaches, air museum, lakes, forests, historical landmarks, nearby lighthouses and historic neighboring cities to draw in the tourists and carry the town through from season to season."

(3)   The correct answer is: **B) Paul Bunyan.**

QUESTION: What famous lumberjack is associated with Oscoda?

EXPLANATION: The answer to this question can be found in lines 3-4: "The town is known as the home of Paul Bunyan. It got that reputation because the first story of Paul Bunyan was printed in its local newspaper."

(4)   The correct answer is: **B) A female lumberjack is referred to as a lumber jill.**

QUESTION: If a man is called a lumberjack, what do you think a female lumberjack is called?

EXPLANATION: The answer is not explicitly stated in the passage, but based on the possible answers provided, lumber jill is a logical guess.

(5)   The correct answer is: **A) Oscoda is known for its famous white sand beaches.**

QUESTION: What kinds of beaches is Oscoda known for?

EXPLANATION: The answer to this question can be found in line 11: "Oscoda now relies on its famous white sand beaches."

Test 2 Mathematics Achievement

(1)   The correct answer is: **A) 30% of the kids in Mr. Evens' class have blond hair.**

EXPLANATION: There are 10 kids in Mr. Evens' class, so each child will represent 10% of the class. The question is what percentage of kids have blond hair. Three kids have blond hair, so if each child is 10% of the class, blond kids make up 30% of the class.

(2)   The correct answer is: **D) The GCF of 3, 9 and 22 is 1.**

EXPLANATION: The only common factor 3, 9 and 22 have in common is the number 1.

(3)   The correct answer is: **A) Every week, Angela runs 36 miles.**

(4)   The correct answer is: **A) The distance is 10 miles.**

EXPLANATION: The total distance of Mark and Murphy's daily walk is 28 miles. The distance from his home to work and from the park to the grocery store is 4 miles each way. Total Miles (28) – Pine to Maple and Sycamore to Birch (4 + 4) = 8 ; 28 – 8 = 20. The distance from Maple to Sycamore and Burch to Pine is equidistant (20 ÷ 2 = 10). So, the other two roads are 10 miles each.

(5)   The correct answer is: **D) $\sqrt{44}$.**

(6)   The correct answer is: **A) 16 is the square root of 256.**

(7)   The correct answer is: **B) The diameter of the circle is 30 inches.**

(8)   The correct answer is: **C) The square root of 16 is 4.**

(9)   The correct answer is: **B) 125,256,000.02.**

(10)   The correct answer is: **A) Fifteen hundred or one thousand five hundred.**

(11)   The correct answer is: **A) 500.025.**

(12)   The correct answer is: **C) $1\frac{5}{8}$**

(13)   The correct answer is: **B) hundredths.**

(14)   The correct answer is: **A) 32%.**

EXPLANATION: The percentage of the whole is 100%. 100% − 60% (flour) = 40% − 8% (wet ingredients) = 32%.

(15)   The correct answer is: **A) 1 in 6.**

EXPLANATION: There are six sides to the dice. So every time you roll the dice you have a 1 in 6 chance of rolling any one number.

(16)   The correct answer is: **C) The animal shelter needs to buy 2 bags of dog food for the first week.**

EXPLANATION: There are 7 dogs at the shelter. The dogs get fed two cups of food twice a day, which means each dog gets 4 cups of food per day. 4 cups of food × 7 days is 28 cups of dog food per dog per week. 7 dogs × 28 cups of dog food per dog per week is 196 cups of dog food for the whole shelter in one week. The shelter needs 2 bags of dog food to get through the week since there are only 184 one-cup servings per bag of dog food.

(17)   The correct answer is: **B) Yes, they would weigh 1,159 pounds and would be light enough to ride in the truck.**

EXPLANATION: 1 ton is equal to 2,000 pounds. Oreo is 506 pounds, Marvin is 96 pounds and Lilly is 957 pounds. There total weight is 506 + 96 + 957 = 1,559 pounds. If the truck can carry up to 2,000 pounds, the animals could all ride in the truck because they are under the weight limit.

(18)   The correct answer is: **D) The average height of the girls is 4 feet 9 inches.**

EXPLANATION: Helen is 4'3", Megan is 5'6", Tasha is 5'2" and Danielle is 4'9". (4'3" + 5'6"+ 5'2" + 4'9" = 18'20" = 19'8"). Divide 19'8" by the number of girls (4) and the average is 4 feet 9 inches.

(19)   The correct answer is: **D) 732.**

EXPLANATION: $(a + b) \times (b - c) = ?$ $(12 + 49) \times (49 - 37) = ?$ $(61) \times (12) = 732$.

(20)   The correct answer is: **B) 7.**

EXPLANATION: $4 + 9 + 6 - 12 = c$.

(21)   The correct answer is: **D) Sam's package will cost him $57.50 after taxes.**

EXPLANATION: $5.46 + $1.50 + 0.79 +$45= $52.75 + 9% tax = $57.50.

(22)   The correct answer is: **A) 789,700**

(23)   The correct answer is: **C) 18π.**

(24)   The correct answer is: **A) Hundreds.**

(25)   The correct answer is: **A) The area of Tristan's deck is 540 square feet.**

EXPLANATION: To find the area of the deck, multiply width by length: 15 × 36 = 540 square feet.

(26)   The correct answer is: **B) The area of Jason's fishing cabin is 33,600 square feet.**

EXPLANATION: To find the area of the cabin, multiply width by length: 168 × 200 = 33,600 square feet.

(27)   The correct answer is: **D) Anna sold 123 pies.**

EXPLANATION: Anna and her mother made $891.75. Divide the total amount earned by the price of each pie to get the number of pies sold. $891.75 ÷ $7.25 = 123 pies.

(28)   The correct answer is: **B) 87.**

EXPLANATION: 125 ÷ 5 = 25, so 25 + 47.25 + 14.386 = 86.636. Rounded to the nearest whole number, 86.636 is 87.

(29)   The correct answer is: **B) 1/4, 1/3, 1/2 .**

EXPLANATION: 1/4 is the smallest of the three fractions 1:4. 1/3 is the middle fraction 1:3. 1/2 is half of a whole, which makes it the largest of the fractions.

(30)   The correct answer is: **A) Thousands.**

Test 3: Verbal Reasoning

In the Verbal Reasoning section of this practice test, you will find practice questions that require you to do one of two things. You will either choose the **synonym** that means the same or similar thing to the **CAPITALIZED** word beside each numbered question, or you will be asked to choose from the multiple-choice answers to select the word or phrase that most logically **completes the sentence** you're given.

Synonym Directions: For the following practice test questions, read the **CAPITALIZED** word carefully. Choose the multiple-choice answer that means the same or close to the same as the **CAPITALIZED** word.

(1)   MAJORITY

(A)   minimalist

(B)   unpopular

(C)   preponderance

(D)   uncommon

(2)   NARRATOR

(A)   audience

(B)   subdue

(C)   reference

(D)   chronicler

(3)   OBJECTIVE

(A)   intention

(B)   pointless

(C)   unencumbered

(D)   prejudice

(4)   PEDESTRIAN

(A)   unique

(B)   humdrum

(C)   inspired

(D)   exciting

(5)   REFUGE

(A)   deserted

(B)   unencumbered

(C)   asylum

(D)   destitute

(6)   SAUNTER

(A)   marathon

(B)   gallop

(C)   relay

(D)   mosey

(7)   TANGIBLE

(A)   corporeal

(B)   untouchable

(C)   intangible

(D)   undefined

(8)   UNIQUE

(A)   replicate

(B)   exclusive

(C)   common

(D)   generic

(9) VISUAL

(A) blinding

(B) uncharacteristic

(C) illustration

(D) translucent

(10) WILDERNESS

(A) suburban

(B) vestibule

(C) cityscape

(D) boondocks

(11) ARROGANT

(A) egotistical

(B) subordinate

(C) unimportant

(D) humble

(12) BUNGLE

(A) manage

(B) ruin

(C) succeed

(D) empower

(13) CAMPAIGN

(A) surrender

(B) congregate

(C) canvass

(D) statuesque

(14)   DEPRIVE

(A)   invest

(B)   provide

(C)   palatable

(D)   dispossess

(15)   EVOLVE

(A)   progress

(B)   devolve

(C)   retrieve

(D)   recede

(16)   FEEBLE

(A)   effective

(B)   meager

(C)   strong

(D)   efficient

(17)   GENERATE

(A)   deprivation

(B)   unproductive

(C)   breed

(D)   flatulent

Sentence Completion Directions: For the following practice test questions, choose the answer that logically completes each sentence. Then read the question to yourself again with the answer you've chosen to ensure that it still makes sense to you, before moving on to the next one.

Test 3 Sentence Completion

(1)   Seeing the high score on my latest exam _____ me that I was doing well.

(A)   disheartened

(B)   crestfallen

(C)   daunted

(D)   reassured

(2)   We got the new _____ for our company and it filled me with pride to see my name on the letterhead.

(A)   stationery

(B)   signage

(C)   materials

(D)   promotions

(3)   The _____ weather was warm and breezy as I walked along the shore.

(A)   arctic

(B)   tropical

(C)   desert

(D)   rainforest

(4)   My children were being unruly at the restaurant, _____.

(A)   so they were rewarded with ice cream when we got home.

(B)   so we ordered dessert to celebrate.

(C)   so they went to bed without dessert.

(D)   so they got to stay up late for their behavior.

(5)   By feeling each item in the bag, the students were able to guess the ____ size and shape of the objects.

(A)   exact

(B)   precise

(C)   approximate

(D)   scrupulous

(6)   During the blizzard, the ____.

(A)   wind and sand made it impossible to drive anywhere.

(B)   rain and debris made it impossible to drive anywhere.

(C)   bright and clear sky made it impossible to drive anywhere.

(D)   snow and ice made it impossible to drive anywhere.

(7)   The judge assigned a guardian when ____.

(A)   my grandfather became too confused to make decisions.

(B)   my sister hit a light post on her way home from work.

(C)   my father ran a red light.

(D)   my adoption was finalized.

(8)   The forest was dark and ____, with bare tree branches, pointy shadows and odd noises as I walked home that night.

(A)   quaint

(B)   eerie

(C)   resplendent

(D)   whimsical

(9)   My favorite movie quote is "Resistance is ____."

(A)   aspire

(B)   upheaval

(C)   futile

(D)   descending

(10)   The computers will ____ new exams each week.

(A)   filter

(B)   separate

(C)   tabulate

(D)   generate

(11)   I can't find the ____ of the burning smell.

(A)   source

(B)   catalyst

(C)   direction

(D)   arson

(12)   The judge issued a ____ and desist order.

(A)   sustain

(B)   cease

(C)   persist

(D)   unceasing

(13)   My brother and I had a heated ____ when he broke my favorite toy.

(A)   discussion

(B)   consultation

(C)   argument

(D)   debate

(14)   This exam will help to ____ us on a level field.

(A)   contrast

(B)   collate

(C)   juxtapose

(D)   evaluate

(15)   Making the Dean's List is one of the highest ____ you can attain at our school.

(A)   achievements

(B)   certifications

(C)   clarifications

(D)   validations

(16)   My mother would ____ anchovy pizza and ice cream each time she got pregnant.

(A)   detest

(B)   crave

(C)   abhor

(D)   consider

(17)   My history project was ____ on Friday.

(A)   dew

(B)   due

(C)   do

(D)   None of the above.

Test 3: Quantitative Reasoning

Directions: In this section, you will find a variety of questions that test your quantitative reasoning skills. The questions in this section will involve a variety of mathematical skills including mathematical operations, measurements, probability, logical reasoning and more. You will be provided with additional information such as graphs or shapes if they are needed for a specific question.

Read each of the questions and answers carefully. If unsure, consider what information is provided with each possible answer. Eliminate the answers you know don't fit until you reach the most logical answer.

(1)   There are 15 houses on the block. Two are red, four are blue, one is white, two are beige and the rest are gray. How many houses are gray?

(A)   There are 9 houses that are gray.

(B)   There are 11 houses that are gray.

(C)   There are 4 houses that are gray.

(D)   There are 6 houses that are gray.

(2)   What do you achieve by adding a set of numbers together and dividing the sum by the number of numbers in the set?

(A)   Mode

(B)   Average

(C)   Percentage

(D)   Median

(3)   What is the first step in solving a calculation involving fractions?

(A)   Multiplying the fractions.

(B)   Ensuring that the denominators are the same.

(C)   Dividing the fractions.

(D)   Adding the numerators.

(4)   How is the word problem "the product of 7 and 14" expressed as an expression?

(A) $7 + 14$

(B) $7 \div 14$

(C) $7 - 14$

(D) 7×14

(5)   If Alisha works Monday, Wednesday, Thursday, Friday and Sunday, how many days out of the week does she work?

(A)   Alisha works 2 out of 7 days of the week.

(B)   Alisha works 5 out of 7 days of the week.

(C)   Alisha works 3 out of 5 days of the week.

(D)   Alisha works 4 out of 7 days of the week.

(6)   The hotel is holding a gala in its main ballroom. The ballroom can hold up to 500 guests. Tickets are $50 a person. If the hotel has sold $15,000 in tickets so far, roughly how many tickets are still left to sell?

(A)   There are 400 tickets left to be sold.

(B)   There are 300 tickets left to be sold.

(C)   There are 200 tickets left to be sold.

(D)   There are 100 tickets left to be sold.

(7)   Lisa is buying new curtains for her house. She bought eight sets of curtains on sale today. If Lisa has 20 windows in her house, how many sets of curtains does she still need to buy?

(A)   Lisa needs to purchase 10 more sets of curtains.

(B)   Lisa needs to purchase 11 more sets of curtains.

(C)   Lisa needs to purchase 12 more sets of curtains.

(D)   Lisa needs to purchase 13 more sets of curtains.

(8)   Milo is going scuba diving. His oxygen tank has a three-hour tank when it's full. If Milo's tank is only two-thirds of the way full, how long can Milo dive before he needs a fresh tank?

(A)   Milo can dive for 9 hours before he will need a fresh oxygen tank.

(B)   Milo can dive for 6 hours before he will need a fresh oxygen tank.

(C)   Milo can dive for 2 hours before he will need a fresh oxygen tank.

(D)   Milo can dive for 1 hour before he will need a fresh oxygen tank.

(9)   Marissa got into an accident on her way home. The body shop says it will cost $154.36 to repair the light of her car, $698.23 for the quarter panel and $229 for the bumper. Rounding to the nearest ten, what will the cost of Marissa's repairs be?

(A)   Marissa's repairs will cost around $1,070.

(B)   Marissa's repairs will cost around $1,080.

(C)   Marissa's repairs will cost around $1,090.

(D)   Marissa's repairs will cost around $1,101.

(10)   George and Tyner are splitting the cost of their fishing cabin evenly. If George paid $471 for his share, what is the total cost of the cabin, rounding to the nearest hundred?

(A)   The total cost of the fishing cabin is $900.

(B)   The total cost of the fishing cabin is $800.

(C)   The total cost of the fishing cabin is $700.

(D)   The total cost of the fishing cabin is $600.

(11)   If Steven is driving 45 miles per hour and he leaves the house at 8 a.m., how many hours will it take to arrive in Morton, 180 miles away?

(A)   It will take Steven 2 hours to get to Morton.

(B)   It will take Steven 4 hours to get to Morton.

(C)   It will take Steven 6 hours to get to Morton.

(D)   It will take Steven 8 hours to get to Morton.

(12)   Kelly orders a pizza for her roommate Megan, her friend Stacy, and herself. The pizza comes in 8 slices. If Megan has three slices, Stacy has two slices and Kelly has the rest, what fraction of the pizza did each of the girls get?

(A)   Megan had 3/8 of the pizza, Stacy had 2/8 of the pizza and Kelly had 3/8 of the pizza.

(B)   Megan, Stacy and Kelly each had 1/3 of the pizza.

(C)   Megan and Stacy ate half of the pizza and Kelly had half of the pizza.

(D)   Each of the girls had 1/4 of the pizza for themselves.

(13)   Mark is six and his mom pays him in pennies every time he helps around the house. If Mark earned $0.06 on Monday, $0.12 on Tuesday, $0.53 Wednesday, $0.22 on Thursday and $0.76 on Friday, how much did he earn on Saturday to give him a total of $2.44?

(A)   Mark earned 43 cents on Saturday.

(B)   Mark earned 38 cents on Saturday.

(C)   Mark earned 27 cents on Saturday.

(D)   Mark earned 75 cents on Saturday.

(14)   The school is doing a school-wide book reading. Each student receives a copy of the same book and will read 12 pages a day. If everyone starts reading on Wednesday and students only read Monday through Friday when school is in session, how many pages will a student have read by the following Thursday?

(A)   A student will have read 108 pages by next Thursday.

(B)   A student will have read 36 pages by next Thursday.

(C)   A student will have read 84 pages by next Thursday.

(D)   A student will have read 24 pages by next Thursday.

(15)   There are 24 pages of study material for James to review. If he reads 1/4 of the material each night for 4 nights, how many pages will he have to review each night?

(A)   James needs to review 4 pages of study material each night.

(B)   James needs to review 6 pages of study material each night.

(C)   James needs to review 12 pages of study material each night.

(D)   James needs to review 5 pages of study material each night.

(16)   There is a jar of 26 bouncy balls on Ms. Nevel's desk that no one can see clearly. On the first day of school, she asked students to each guess how many balls were in the jar. There are 26 students in her class. Each student must guess differently from other students. If everyone takes a guess, what is the ratio of guessing correctly in contrast to the rest of the class?

(A)   Every student has a 1 in 26 chance of guessing correctly or a ratio of 1:26.

(B)   Every student has a 26 in 26 chance of guessing correctly or a ratio of 26:26.

(C)   Every student has a 13 in 26 chance of guessing correctly or a ratio of 13:14.

(D)   Every student has a 50/50 chance of guessing correctly or a ratio of 50:50.

(17)   If Anna collects stones on her way home each day, collecting two or three a day for 10 days, what is the least and most amount of stones she could have collected?

(A)   Anna collected between 10 and 20 stones.

(B)   Anna collected between 20 and 30 stones.

(C)   Anna collected between 35 and 45 stones.

(D)   Anna collected between 30 and 40 stones.

(18)   The fruit and veggie platter at the grocery store has six kinds of fruit and four types of veggies. What fraction set correctly expresses that data?

(A)   The platter contains 6/10 fruit and 4/10 veggies.

(B)   The platter contains 1/2 fruit and 1/2 veggies.

(C)   The platter contains 3/4 fruit and 1/4 veggies.

(D)   The platter contains 4/10 fruit and 6/10 veggies.

(19)   The dogs get walked three times a day. Their first walk is a quarter-mile, the second is two and a half miles and the third walk is a quarter-mile. How many miles do the dogs get walked each day?

(A)   The dogs walk 2 ½ miles each day.

(B)   The dogs walk 4 miles each day.

(C)   The dogs walk 3 ½ miles each day.

(D)   The dogs walk 3 miles each day.

(20)   Aaron swims 15 laps a day, three days a week at the gym. How many laps does Aaron swim each week?

(A)   Aaron swims 15 laps a week.

(B)   Aaron swims 30 laps a week.

(C)   Aaron swims 45 laps a week.

(D)   Aaron swims 50 laps a week.

(21)   Heather is crocheting a blanket for her niece. The blanket is pink, white and chocolate-colored. Heather does three rows of chocolate, six rows of white and twelve rows of pink, then repeats the pattern. If there are 84 rows altogether, how many rows are pink?

(A)   There will be 48 pink rows on the blanket.

(B)   There will be 24 pink rows on the blanket.

(C)   There will be 12 pink rows on the blanket.

(D)   There will be 36 pink rows on the blanket.

(22)   There are five women in Sheena's department and eight men. Roughly what percentage of her workforce is male?

(A)   Sheena's workforce is made up of around 32% men.

(B)   Sheena's workforce is made up of around 42% men.

(C)   Sheena's workforce is made up of around 52% men.

(D)   Sheena's workforce is made up of around 62% men.

(23)   Joseph and Josie have been married for 25 years. If they celebrated their 20th anniversary in 2015, in what year were they married?

(A)   Joseph and Josie were married in 2015.

(B)   Joseph and Josie were married in 2005.

(C)   Joseph and Josie were married in 1995.

(D)   Joseph and Josie were married in 1985.

(24) Beth is 5, Mavis is 12, Dahlia is 14, Trish is 16 and Emma is 18. What is the average age of the girls?

(A) The average age of all five girls is 15 years old.

(B) The average age of all five girls is 13 years old.

(C) The average age of all five girls is 11 years old.

(D) The average age of all five girls is 17 years old.

(25) Mia wants to redo the floors in her rectangular office. If the office is 18 feet by 36 feet, what is the area of her office?

(A) The area of Mia's office is 648 sq. ft.

(B) The area of Mia's office is 650 sq. ft.

(C) The area of Mia's office is 683 sq. ft.

(D) The area of Mia's office is 698 sq. ft.

(26) Parker has 150 matchbox cars. If 100 of his cars fit in his matchbox case, what fraction of his cars will be left out?

(A) 3/1 of his cars will be left out.

(B) 2/10 of his cars will be left out.

(C) 50/100 of his cars will be left out.

(D) 1/3 of his cars will be left out.

(27)   What is the fraction 16/32 in lowest terms?

(A)   1/2

(B)   6/36

(C)   8/32

(D)   3/4

(28)   Alan is cutting a hole in the wall for new windows. If the width of the hole needs to be an inch larger than the width of the window and the window is 43 inches wide, how wide does the hole need to be?

(A)   The hole for the window needs to be 45 inches wide.

(B)   The hole for the window needs to be 41 inches wide.

(C)   The hole for the window needs to be 44 inches wide.

(D)   The hole for the window needs to be 42 inches wide.

(29)   If a ball needs to be filled with 50% more air and the pressure gauge reads 50 psi, how many psi does the ball need to increase to?

(A)   75 psi

(B)   50 psi

(C)   45 psi

(D)   15 psi

(30)   Gage is fixing the classic car his father left him. If the oil he puts in needs to be eighty twenty, which of the following expresses that correctly?

(A) 80×20

(B) $80 - 20$

(C) $80/20$

(D) $80:20$

(31)   There are 15 horses in a field. There are the same numbers of quarter horses as there are palominos, and there are three more Arabians than palominos. If there are 7 Arabians, how many other horses are there?

(A)   There are four palominos and two quarter horses

(B)   There are four quarter horses and four palominos.

(C)   There are ten quarter horses and ten palominos.

(D)   There are ten palominos and thirteen quarter horses.

(32)   The girls are each pitching at softball practice with a dozen balls each. If a dozen = 12 and there are 22 girls pitching, how many balls will be on the field after pitching practice?

(A)   There will be 264 softballs out on the field.

(B)   There will be 232 softballs out on the field.

(C)   There will be 284 softballs out on the field.

(D)   There will be 226 softballs out on the field.

(33)   There are 30 tables at the restaurant and 60 booths. Each table has 1 set and each booth has 1 seat. If there are a total of 100 seats in the restaurant between tables, booths and bar seats, then how many seats are bar seats?

(A)   There are 10 bar seats.

(B)   There are 20 bar seats.

(C)   There are 15 bar seats.

(D)   There are 12 bar seats.

(34)   Horton had to sit on an egg for 5 days. There are 24 hours in a day. If Horton never moved off the egg, how many hours did he sit on the egg keeping it warm?

(A)   Horton sat on the egg for 24 hours.

(B)   Horton sat on the egg for 36 hours.

(C)   Horton sat on the egg for 72 hours.

(D)   Horton sat on the egg for 120 hours.

(35)   Each gift basket gets four muffins, a jumbo cookie and a box of chocolates. If Mina makes 12 baskets, how many muffins will she need to bake?

(A)   Mia will need to make 38 muffins.

(B)   Mia will need to make 48 muffins.

(C)   Mia will need to make 58 muffins.

(D)   Mia will need to make 68 muffins.

(36)   Adam has three friends on his team and is playing a video game online with another team. The other team has one less player than Adam's team. The other team has what percentage of fewer players?

(A)   The other team has 25% fewer players than Adam's team.

(B)   The other team has 50% fewer players than Adam's team.

(C)   The other team has 75% fewer players than Adam's team.

(D)   The other team has 90% fewer players than Adam's team.

(37)   The red team scored 15 points in the first half and 21 points in the second half. The blue team scored five fewer points in the first half than the red team and 12 points more than the red team in the second half. How many points did the blue team score in each half?

(A)   The blue team scored 10 points in the first half and 33 points in the second half.

(B)   The blue team scored 15 points in the first half and 21 points in the second half.

(C)   The blue team and the red team each scored the same number of points in the first and second halves.

(D)   The blue team scored more points in the first half than they did in the second half.

(38)   Alay's room is being painted pink. It takes two 1-gallon jars of white paint and one 1-gallon jar of red paint to make the color she likes. If the room will require 5 gallons of paint, how many gallons of the mix will be needed if it can only be mixed in 3-gallon buckets?

(A)   6 gallons of paint will need to be purchased for Alay's room.

(B)   3 gallons of paint will need to be purchased for Alay's room.

(C)   5 gallons of paint will need to be purchased for Alay's room.

(D)   12 gallons of paint will need to be purchased for Alay's room.

Test 3: Reading Comprehension

Directions: Read each passage that follows carefully. Think about the main points, the tone and feel of the passage, the information presented and anything that you feel the passage might be implying. When you are through reading each passage, carefully read each question and the corresponding answers. Using the information you gained from the passage, choose the correct answer.

Test 3 Passage 1 & Questions:

1. Have you ever wondered about outer space?
2. The people on Earth have been fascinated with space for centuries.
3. On Wednesday, April 10, 2019, science was rocked.
4. We were given our first picture of a black hole.
5. It all started with a team of international astronomers.
6. Together they created the EHT or Event Horizon Telescope.
7. The creation was built on technology we had to take pictures of things far away.
8. The team took what we knew and a dream they had, and built something amazing,
9. creating a network of smaller telescopes to build the EHT.
10. To get the imaging, computer programs and telescopes in line and working properly,
11. they chose two objects to focus on.
12. Those earmarks have been named Sagittarius A* and M87*.
13. The first location, Sagittarius A*, is at the center of our Milky Way Galaxy.
14. It is 26,000 light-years from Earth.
15. The second is M87*, which is in the Gargantuan Elliptical Galaxy.
16. M87* is 53,000,000 light-years away.
17. M87* is said to be larger than Sagittarius A*.
18. The international team worked from eight locations around the world
19. to coordinate on the project.
20. Surprisingly, a black hole isn't a hole at all.
21. It's an object that has so much mass stuffed into a small space
22. that it creates a very powerful gravitational pull.
23. It's so powerful, in fact, that not even light can escape it.
24. Capturing this picture has sparked an even bigger project.
25. The US National Science Foundation is awarding a $12.7 million grant to start the next phase.
26. What they are calling the next-generation EHT or ngEHT will allow them to take real-time
27. videos of the black holes rather than the photographs they are getting now.

Directions: Using the passage above, answer each of the five questions that follow. Refer back to the passage to confirm your answer choices and refresh the details of your memory. The answers to all of the questions will either be in the passage or will require your opinion or point of view, so there is no outside information you need to know.

(1)   What is a black hole?

(A)   A hole in space that sucks in everything that gets close into it.

(B)   A planet that can suck things into it with gravity so they can't get out.

(C)   An object of mass, packed tight, with strong gravity that doesn't let anything escape.

(D)   A hole in space that can take you to other places.

(2)   What galaxy is Sagittarius A* located in?

(A)   Sagittarius A* is located in the Milky Way Galaxy.

(B)   Sagittarius A* is located in the Gargantuan Elliptical Galaxy.

(C)   Sagittarius A* is located in the Andromeda Galaxy.

(D)   Sagittarius A* is located in the Virgo Stellar Stream.

(3)   What galaxy is M87* located in?

(A)   M87* is located in the Milky Way Galaxy.

(B)   M87* is located in the Cartwheel Galaxy.

(C)   M87* is located in the Triangulum Galaxy.

(D)   M87* is located in the Gargantuan Galaxy.

(4)   What are scientists hoping to achieve with the next-generation EHT?

(A)   They are hoping to go into a black hole.

(B)   They are hoping to take clear photographs of the black hole.

(C)   They are hoping to take a real-time video of the black hole.

(D)   They are hoping to travel to the black hole themselves.

(5) How many light-years away is the black hole Sagittarius A*?

(A) Sagittarius A* is 53,000,000 light-years away.

(B) Sagittarius A* is 26,000 light-years away.

(C) Sagittarius A* is 53,000 light-years away.

(D) Sagittarius A* is 26,000,000 light-years away.

Test 3 Passage 2 & Questions:

1.   Today, almost everyone uses the internet, and very few of us give it a second thought.

2.   Today, younger generations don't even know of a time when the internet didn't exist.

3.   I remember that time. I remember when the internet was first rolled out publicly.

4.   Could you imagine not being able to just hop onto Facebook, Instagram or Twitter from your cell phone? Not having Google Maps for directions or the internet to look up

5.   the topic for your class biography project?

6.   I can remember looking at paper maps for directions, having to comb through a card catalog to

7.   find books for school research projects. I remember when cell phones were barely a thing

8.   and when Facebook, Instagram and Twitter didn't even exist.

9.   So, how did we get our wonderful World Wide Web?

10.   You should thank Sir Tim Berners-Lee.

11.   Sir Tim Berners-Lee is an English engineer and computer scientist from London, England.

12.   What is now the internet was his brainchild.

13.   After graduating from Oxford University, in Oxford, England,

14.   Tim took a job as a software engineer for a company called CERN.

15.   CERN is a particle physics laboratory.

16.   Their accelerator was highly sought-after at the time and scientists from all over the globe

17.   would travel to CERN, near Geneva, Switzerland, to use the accelerator.

18.   Tim noticed a problem for these scientists though.

19.   There was a huge problem communicating and sharing information with so much distance.

20.   So, in 1990, Tim approached his boss with a proposal to create a better way.

21.   While his project wasn't actually a company project,

22.   he was given permission and time to work on his idea.

23.   Tim used a NeXT computer, created by Steve Jobs, to start his project in September 1990.

24.   By October he had made huge strides in his programming,

25.   creating three core formats that we still use today.

26.   Those programs are HTML, URI (also called URL) and HTTP.

27.   By the end of that same year, Tim opened his first web page on the internet.

28.   The internet originally was open just to CERN.

29.	In January 1991, it was opened up to other scientific facilities.

30.	Then in August 1991, it was finally opened to the public.

31.	Seeing the true potential of his creation and its possibilities,

32.	Tim and others approached CERN about making the base coding available to everyone,

33.	without charge or permission, for the rest of the existence of the World Wide Web.

34.	The agreement was made and finally announced in 1993.

35.	In 1994, Tim left CERN and moved on to MIT in Cambridge, Massachusetts.

36.	There he founded W3C or the World Wide Web Consortium.

37.	He and the rest of the consortium developed a community standard for the web.

38.	Today, Tim is still the director of the W3C.

39.	Over the years since its inception, the internet has grown, creating a technological universe,

40.	connecting everyone and everything to it with just the tips of our fingers.

Directions: Using the passage above, answer each of the five questions that follow. Refer back to the passage to confirm your answer choices and refresh the details of your memory. The answers to all of the questions will either be in the passage or will require your opinion or point of view, so there is no outside information you need to know.

(1)	Where is Sir Tim Berners-Lee from?

(A)	Sir Tim Berners-Lee is from Geneva, Switzerland.

(B)	Sir Tim Berners-Lee is from Cambridge, Massachusetts.

(C)	Sir Tim Berners-Lee is from London, England.

(D)	Sir Tim Berners-Lee is from Oxford, England.

(2)	What three formats did Tim create for the internet that we still use now?

(A)	The three formats still used today that Tim created are the World Wide Web.

(B)	The three formats still used today that Tim created are HTML, URL and HTTP.

(C)	The three formats still used today that Tim created are the World Wide Web Consortium.

(D)	The three formats still used today that Tim created are the W3C.

(3)   What early Steve Jobs' creation did Tim use when creating the World Wide Web?

(A)   When creating the World Wide Web, Tim used Steve Jobs' NeXT computer.

(B)   When creating the World Wide Web, Tim used Steve Jobs' Mac computer.

(C)   When creating the World Wide Web, Tim used Steve Jobs' Dell computer.

(D)   When creating the World Wide Web, Tim used Steve Jobs' MIT computer.

(4)   What problem did Tim see while working for CERN that prompted him to create the internet?

(A)   Tim could see that there was a disconnect for scientists sharing information and communicating.

(B)   Tim could see that there was a disconnect for scientists traveling to Geneva to use the CERN particle accelerator.

(C)   Tim could see that there was a disconnect for creating a community standard for web use.

(D)   All of the above.

(5)   What agreement did Tim and others collaborate with CERN on?

(A)   They collaborated to develop the World Wide Web.

(B)   They collaborated to make the internet available to everyone without charge or permission.

(C)   They collaborated to develop a community standard.

(D)   They collaborated to move to MIT to create the World Wide Web Consortium.

Test 3 Passage 3 & Questions:

1. You are clear and you are dark.
2. Maybe you are black or maybe you are blue.
3. Either way your face will glow with dancing lights upon it.
4. High above me your glowing ball sits,
5. casting down around me a glow.
6. Scorpio plays and Gemini dances,
7. while Libra makes a happy home.
8. The Big and Little Dippers play games of tag.
9. From time to time, cotton balls float by,
10. hiding you from my sight when they do,
11. and sometimes your glowing ball hides too.
12. When the sun comes out to play,
13. all my sky friends hide away.
14. But when the sun sets, you come again.
15. When you are here, I do not fear.
16. You chase away the dark, dark night.
17. You are my perfect nightlight,
18. Watching over me from high above.
19. I know that I am always loved.
20. For when I'm in bed at night, looking up at such a sight,
21. my dad abroad can look up too.
22. We see the same moon, me and you.

Directions: Using the passage above, answer each of the five questions that follow. Refer back to the passage to confirm your answer choices and refresh the details of your memory. The answers to all of the questions will either be in the passage or will require your opinion or point of view, so there is no outside information you need to know.

(1) What is the poem talking about?

(A) The poem is talking about the night sky.

(B) The poem is talking about the moon.

(C) The poem is talking about star constellations.

(D) All of the above.

(2)   What are Scorpio, Gemini, Libra, the Little Dipper and the Big Dipper?

(A)   Fireflies

(B)   Stars that make pictures

(C)   The moon

(D)   Animals

(3)   What does the line "We see the same moon, me and you," mean?

(A)   That the moon is everywhere.

(B)   That "me and you" are next to each other looking up at the moon.

(C)   That when you are far apart, you feel together when you both see the moon.

(D)   None of the above.

(4)   What is the "glowing ball" in the poem?

(A)   The glowing ball in the poem is a nightlight.

(B)   The glowing ball in the poem is a star.

(C)   The glowing ball in the poem is the moon.

(D)   The glowing ball in the poem is a planet.

(5)   What do "cotton balls" represent in the poem?

(A)   Cotton balls in the poem refer to clouds.

(B)   Cotton balls in the poem refer to the grass.

(C)   Cotton balls in the poem refer to fog.

(D)   Cotton balls in the poem refer to the moon.

Test 3 Passage 4 & Questions:

1.   The Smithsonian National Zoo was founded in 1889.

2.   The zoo is located in Rock Creek Park in Washington, D.C.

3.   It's home to more than 2,700 animals whose homes are spread out across 163 acres.

4.   The primate enclosure found its permanent residence at the National Zoo on April 15, 1981.

5.   Gorillas, apes, orangutans, lemurs and monkeys are some of the animals that make their

6.   home here in the Great Ape House permanently.

7.   The Small Mammal House is home to more than 35 species of small mammals

8.   and has been a permanent home there since April 1, 1983.

9.   On August 19, 1992, the Cheetah Conservation Station was added and is home to a multitude of

10.   animals in addition to the cheetah, including zebras, red river hogs, gazelles and oryx.

11.   Between 1992 and 1998, Amazonia, Think Tank and Big Cats exhibits were also added to the zoo.

12.   On June 12, 2004, the Kids' Farm was added. This exhibit lets kids get up close and personal

13.   with farm animals including cows, donkeys, chickens, hogs, alpacas and more.

14.   The Kids' Farm also does demonstrations and educational events for kids throughout the day.

15.   From 2006-2014, the Asia Trail, the Elephant Trail, the American Trail and the American

16.   Bison exhibits found permanent homes within the National Zoo.

17.   The Electric Fish Demonstration Lab, Reptile Discovery Center and Naked Mole Rats on the Move exhibits are all on indefinite display in the Smithsonian National Zoo right now.

18.   The zoo is also running a Celebrate Smokey: 75 Years of Fighting Wildfires special exhibit

19.   on May 22nd, 2020.

20.   The Smithsonian National Zoo is open 364 days a year, only closing for Christmas Day.

21.   So you can go see all of their spectacular animals almost any day of the year!

Directions: Using the passage above, answer each of the five questions that follow. Refer back to the passage to confirm your answer choices and refresh the details of your memory. The answers to all of the questions will either be in the passage or will require your opinion or point of view, so there is no outside information you need to know.

(1)   When was the National Zoo founded?

(A)   The National Zoo was founded in 1889.

(B)   The National Zoo was founded in 1981.

(C)   The National Zoo was founded in 1998.

(D)   The National Zoo was founded in 2019.

(2)   What was the first animal enclosure to find a permanent home at the zoo?

(A)   The first permanent animal enclosure was the Great Ape House.

(B)   The first permanent animal enclosure was the Cheetah Conservation Station.

(C)   The first permanent animal enclosure was the Asia Trail.

(D)   The first permanent animal enclosure was the Amazonia.

(3)   What exhibit was added on June 12, 2004?

(A)   Amazonia was added on June 12, 2004.

(B)   Think Tank was added on June 12, 2004.

(C)   Great Cats was added on June 12, 2004.

(D)   The Kids' Farm was added on June 12, 2004.

(4)   What special exhibit is currently on display until May 22nd?

(A)   The 75 Years of Fighting Wildfires exhibit is on display on May 22nd.

(B)   The Naked Mole Rats on the Move exhibit is on display until May 22nd.

(C)   The Electric Fish Discovery Lab exhibit is on display until May 22nd.

(D)   None of the above.

(5)   Where is the National Zoo located?

(A)   The National Zoo is located in Central Park.

(B)   The National Zoo is located in Peel Mansion Park.

(C)   The National Zoo is located in Orchards Park.

(D)   The National Zoo is located in Rock Creek Park.

Test 3 Passage 5 & Questions:

1.   The Great Lakes are the largest interconnecting freshwater body of lakes on Earth
2.   by area and the second-largest by volume, with a surface area of 94,250 square miles.
3.   The Great Lakes are made up of Lake Superior, Lake Michigan, Lake Huron,
4.   Lake Erie and Lake Ontario.
5.   Lake Michigan is the only one of the Great Lakes that is located completely in the
6.   United States, while the others border both the United States and Canada.
7.   These five lakes make up what is known as the Great Lakes Waterway and by combined volume
8.   make up 21 percent of the world's surface freshwater.
9.   Though the lakes each have their own water basin, they are all interconnecting.
10.   The Great Lakes are also connected to thousands of smaller inland lakes
11.   and have more than 35,000 islands scattered through.
12.   The Great Lakes meet the Atlantic Ocean through the Saint Lawrence Seaway.
13.   Ships must be small enough to move through the lock of the Saint Lawrence Seaway
14.   in order to access the Great Lakes.
15.   Those that can access the Great Lakes are able to move among all five Great Lakes and travel back to sea as well.
16.   The Great Lakes are often referred to as the inland sea.
17.   They acquired this title because of the behavior of the lakes.
18.   They have rolling waves, strong currents, are very deep, have far-off horizons like the oceans
19.   and sustain strong winds. These behaviors mimic those of our oceans.

Directions: Using the passage above, answer each of the five questions that follow. Refer back to the passage to confirm your answer choices and refresh the details of your memory. The answers to all of the questions will either be in the passage or will require your opinion or point of view, so there is no outside information you need to know.

(1)   How many lakes make up the Great Lakes?

(A)   The Great Lakes are made up of thousands of lakes.

(B)   The Great Lakes are made up of five lakes.

(C)   The Great Lakes are made up of thirty-five thousand lakes.

(D)   The Great Lakes are made up of one lake.

(2)   Which Great Lake is the only one wholly in the United States?

(A)   Lake Huron is the only lake wholly in the United States.

(B)   Lake Superior is the only lake wholly in the United States.

(C)   Lake Michigan is the only lake wholly in the United States.

(D)   Lake Erie is the only lake wholly in the United States.

(3)   What allows ships to move between the Great Lakes and the ocean?

(A)   The Panama Canal allows ships to move between the Great Lakes and the ocean.

(B)   The locks allow ships to move between the Great Lakes and the ocean.

(C)   The inland lakes allow ships to move between the Great Lakes and the ocean.

(D)   The island allows ships to move between the Great Lakes and the ocean.

(4)   What country do the Great Lakes border in addition to the U.S.?

(A)   The Great Lakes also border the country of Alaska.

(B)   The Great Lakes also border the country of the Netherlands.

(C)   The Great Lakes also border the country of Canada.

(D)   The Great Lakes also border the country of Mexico.

(5)   What percentage of freshwater surface do the Great Lakes make up on Earth?

(A)   The Great Lakes make up 21% of Earth's freshwater surface.

(B)   The Great Lakes make up 94,250% of Earth's freshwater surface.

(C)   The Great Lakes make up 35,000% of Earth's freshwater surface.

(D)   None of the above.

Test 3 Mathematics Achievement

Directions: In this Mathematics Achievement practice test you will find a variety of mathematical questions that test your math skills as well as the information you have learned. The questions may include addition, subtraction, multiplication and division, as well as square roots, geometry, measurements, probability and overall problem-solving.

Read each question carefully. Then read each of the multiple-choice questions that follow. Choose the answer that correctly solves each question, word problem or equation. On your official exam, you will be allowed to use the space in your workbook to solve the equations. With that in mind, you may use scratch paper to work the equations in this study guide.

(1)   Mitchell and Martha are making cookies for their school bake sale. They made 100 cookies altogether. Twenty-five cookies are peanut butter, 25 are chocolate chip, 10 are oatmeal, 10 are M&M, 15 are thumbprint and 15 are turtle cookies. What percentage of cookies are M&M or turtle cookies?

(A)   5% of the cookies are M&M or turtle cookies.

(B)   15% of the cookies are M&M or turtle cookies.

(C)   50% of the cookies are M&M or turtle cookies.

(D)   25% of the cookies are M&M or turtle cookies.

(2)   Chris drives six miles to work each day and another six miles back home from work each day. He stops by the grocery store on his way home three nights a week which adds an additional seven miles to his trip home on those days. How many miles does Chris drive in a five-day workweek if all the driving is only done on workdays?

(A)   Chris drives a total of 65 miles each workweek.

(B)   Chris drives a total of 58 miles each workweek.

(C)   Chris drives a total of 44 miles each workweek.

(D)   Chris drives a total of 81 miles each workweek.

(3)   What is the GCF of 16, 32 and 64?

(A)   The GCF of 16, 32 and 64 is 8.

(B)   The GCF of 16, 32 and 64 is 16.

(C)   The GCF of 16, 32 and 64 is 9.

(D)   The GCF of 16, 32 and 64 is 32.

(4)   Which of the word problems expresses $\sqrt{49}$?

(A)   The square root of forty-nine.

(B)   Four is greater than or equal to forty-nine.

(C)   Four divided by nine.

(D)   The absolute value of four and nine is forty-nine.

(5)   12 is the square root of which number?

(A)   12 is the square root of 144.

(B)   12 is the square root of 112.

(C)   12 is the square root of 156.

(D)   12 is the square root of 162.

(6)   What equation do you use to find the area (A) of a rectangle?

(A)   A = ½ (base + top) height

(B)   A = width × length

(C) $A = \pi r^2$

(D)   A = base × height

(7)   What is the square root of 49?

(A)   7 is the square root of 49.

(B)   14 is the square root of 49.

(C)   12 is the square root of 49.

(D)   9 is the square root of 49.

(8)   Which number written below matches 27,456,987?

(A)   Twenty-seven thousand, forty-five hundred six, ninety-eight seven

(B)   Twenty-seven million, four hundred fifty-six thousand, nine hundred eighty-seven

(C)   Twenty-seven, four hundred fifty-six, nine hundred eighty-seven

(D)   Twenty-seven million, four hundred fifty-six, nine hundred eighty-seven

(9)   Which of the following answers is the correct numerical way to write five thousand, two hundred twenty-nine dollars and sixty-two cents?

(A) $50,229.62

(B) $5,229,062.00

(C) $5,229.26

(D) $5,229.62

(10)   In the number 78,9<u>6</u>4, what place value is the number six in?

(A)   Tens

(B)   Ones

(C)   Hundreds

(D)   Thousands

(11)   Which of the following answers correctly shows twenty and two-thirds?

(A) $\frac{20}{23}$

(B) $20\frac{2}{3}$

(C) $23\frac{1}{20}$

(D)   20.23

(12)   In the number 354.1<u>6</u>, what place value is the number one in?

(A)   Tenths

(B)   Tens

(C)   Thousandths

(D)   Tens

(13)   How do you write 60% as a fraction?

(A) $\dfrac{6}{100}$

(B) $60\dfrac{1}{10}$

(C) $\dfrac{60}{100}$

(D) $\dfrac{1}{60}$

(14)   Alan is playing Monopoly with seven of his friends and they are equally good at playing the game. Each person has what percent chance of winning?

(A)   Each player has a 10% chance of winning.

(B)   Each player has a 12.5% chance of winning.

(C)   Each player has a 13% chance of winning.

(D)   Each player has a 15.5% chance of winning.

(15)   Is 4,682 + 496 greater than, less than or equal to 3,329 + 1,204?

(A)   >

(B)   ≤

(C)   <

(D)   ≠

(16)   What expression correctly shows forty-five multiplied by ten is greater than two hundred twenty divided by two?

(A) $45 \times 10 \leq 220 \div 2$

(B) $45 \times 5 \geq 222 \div 10$

(C) $45 \times 10 > 220 \div 2$

(D) $45 > 220$

(17)   Marissa runs six miles through the woods, four miles on the beach and six miles through town to get back home. She makes the same run four days a week. Which calculation shows how Marissa figures out how many miles she runs each day?

(A) $6 + 4 + 6 = 16$ miles

(B) $(6 + 4 + 6)\, 4 = 64$ miles

(C) $(6 \times 4) + (4 \times 4) + (6 \times 4) = 64$ miles

(D) $4 + 6\,(4 + 4)\,6 + 4 = 296$ miles

(18)   Use $a = 12$ and $b = 49$ to find the value of: $(b \div 7) - (a \div 3) + (37 \times 3) = $ ___?

(A)   114

(B)   116

(C)   118

(D)   120

(19)   Solve for c: $24 \times c + 9 = 105$

(A) $c = 3$

(B) $c = 4$

(C) $c = 6$

(D) $c = 12$

(20)   There are 240 fifth graders in our middle school and 260 sixth graders. What is the ratio of sixth graders to fifth graders?

(A)   There are 9 fifth graders to every 11 sixth graders or a 9:11 ratio.

(B)   There are 13 sixth graders to every 12 fifth graders or a 13:12 ratio.

(C)   There are 15 fifth graders to every 14 sixth graders or a 15:14 ratio.

(D)   There are 17 sixth graders to every 16 fifth graders or a 17:16 ratio.

(21)   Round the number 1,547,698,321 to the nearest ten million.

(A)   1,547,700,000

(B)   1,547,699,321

(C)   1,550,000,000

(D)   1,540,000,000

(22)   What is the GCF of 18, 36 and 63?

(A)   The GCF of 18, 36 and 63 is 3.

(B)   The GCF of 18, 36 and 63 is 6.

(C)   The GCF of 18, 36 and 63 is 9.

(D)   The GCF of 18, 36 and 63 is 12.

(23)   Choose the answer that correctly expresses two hundred fifty-two dollars and fifteen cents.

(A) $215.52

(B) $215.00

(C) $200.00

(D) $252.15

(24)   Solve for a: $64 \div a = 4$

(A) $a = 14$

(B) $a = 15$

(C) $a = 16$

(D) $a = 17$

(25)   Write the number 70,450,987,625 in expanded form.

(A)   70,000,000,000 + 400,000,000 + 50,000,000 + 900,000 + 80,000 + 7,000 + 600 + 20 + 5

(B)   700,000,000 + 000 + 40,000,000,000 + 5,000,000 + 9,000 + 800 + 60 + 20 + 50

(C)   7,000,000 + 400,000 + 50,000 + 9,000 + 800 + 700 + 600 + 200 + 50

(D)   700,000,000,000,000 + 400,000,000 + 50,000,000 + 9000,000 + 80,000 + 7,000 + 600 + 20 + 5

(26)   The men on the Jamaican basketball team are extremely tall. Alan is 6 inches taller than Scott, Scott is 3 inches shorter than Dan and Dan is 8 inches taller than Travis. If Travis is 6 feet 4 inches tall, how tall are the rest of the men?

(A)   Alan is 6 feet tall and Scott and Dan are both 7 feet tall.

(B)   Alan is 5 feet 3 inches tall, Scott is 5 feet 9 inches tall and Dan is 6 feet tall.

(C)   Alan is 7 feet 3 inches tall, Scott is 6 feet 9 inches tall and Dan is 7 feet tall.

(D)   Alan is 7 meters 3 centimeters tall, Scott is 6 meters 9 centimeters tall and Dan is 7 meters tall.

(27)   Kate has 12 goody bags for her party. She has 7 made up for female guests and 5 made up for male guests. What percentage of guests are male, rounded to the nearest whole number?

(A)   58% of Kate's party guests are male.

(B)   57% of Kate's party guests are male.

(C)   42% of Kate's party guests are male.

(D)   43% of Kate's party guests are male.

(28)   Melissa is making 100 flower arrangements to sell for Valentine's Day. Thirty-six arrangements are roses, 25 arrangements are carnations and 12 arrangements are daisies. The rest are wildflowers. How many of the arrangements are wildflowers?

(A)   37 wildflower arrangements

(B)   61 wildflower arrangements

(C)   27 wildflower arrangements

(D)   48 wildflower arrangements

(29) Solve for *a*: $a(53 + 86) = 1{,}668$

(A) $a = 13$

(B) $a = 12$

(C) $a = 14$

(D) $a = 11$

(30) Complete the calculation: $0.1876 + 1.5876 + 1{,}157.366 + 12.58 = ?$ and round your answer to the nearest hundredth.

(A)   1,171.7212

(B)   171.17

(C)   1,171.72

(D)   1,1717.212

Test 3 Essay Question

Unlike the other portions of your practice test, there is no right or wrong answer for your essay, so this portion of your practice test will not have an answer section.

__Essay Topic__

What is your favorite book and why do you like it so much?

Test 3 Answers – Verbal Reasoning

In this Practice Test Answer Key, you will find the correct answer for each of the questions on Practice Test 3. The correct answer will be followed by an explanation to clarify why that answer is correct.

Test 3 Synonyms – Answers

(1)   The correct answer is: **C) preponderance – prevalence, hold or important part.**

MAJORITY – mass, bulk or best part. The answer that has the closest meaning to MAJORITY is **preponderance.**

(2)   The correct answer is: **D) chronicler – speaker, relater or storyteller.**

NARRATOR – a speaker, storyteller or teller of tales. The answer that has the closest meaning to NARRATOR is **chronicler.**

(3)   The correct answer is: **A) intention – aim, purpose or goal.**

OBJECTIVE – a purpose, goal or reason. The answer that has the closest meaning to OBJECTIVE is **intention.**

(4)   The correct answer is: **B) humdrum – dull, routine, or boring.**

PEDESTRIAN – person on foot, dull or uninspiring. The answer that has the closest meaning to PEDESTRIAN is **humdrum.**

(5)   The correct answer is: **C) asylum – sanctuary, protection or place of safety.**

REFUGE – safe haven, harbor or protection. The answer that has the closest meaning to REFUGE is **asylum.**

(6)   The correct answer is: **D) mosey – to dawdle, stroll or walk slowly.**

SAUNTER – stroll, mosey or walk. The answer that has the closest meaning to SAUNTER is **mosey.**

(7)   The correct answer is: **A) corporeal – bodily or physical.**

TANGIBLE – physical, real or corporeal. The answer that has the closest meaning to TANGIBLE is **corporeal.**

(8)   The correct answer is: **B) exclusive – one of a kind, special or absolute.**

UNIQUE – uncommon, special or individual. The answer that has the closest meaning to UNIQUE is **exclusive.**

(9)   The correct answer is: **C) illustration – picture, image or visual aid.**

VISUAL – something you can see. The answer that has the closest meaning to VISUAL is **illustration.**

(10)   The correct answer is: **D) boondocks – wilds, backwoods or rough country.**

WILDERNESS – wilds or rough country. The answer that has the closest meaning to WILDERNESS is **boondocks.**

(11)   The correct answer is: **A) egotistical – proud, narcissistic and self-centered.**

ARROGANT – overconfident, superior and proud. The answer that has the closest meaning to ARROGANT is **egotistical.**

(12)   The correct answer is: **B) ruin – damage, destroy or wreck.**

BUNGLE – to botch, ruin or do badly. The answer that has the closest meaning to BUNGLE is **ruin.**

(13)   The correct answer is: **C) canvass – to campaign directly with individuals.**

CAMPAIGN – movement, battle or fight. The answer that has the closest meaning to CAMPAIGN is **canvass.**

(14)   The correct answer is: **D) dispossess – strip, take away or deprive.**

DEPRIVE – divest, rob or deny. The answer that has the closest meaning to DEPRIVE is **dispossess.**

(15)   The correct answer is: **A) progress – steps forward, advancement or improvement.**

EVOLVE – develop, grow and advance. The answer has the closest meaning to EVOLVE is **progress.**

(16)   The correct answer is: **B) meager – not enough, too little and inadequate.**

FEEBLE – meager, frail or weak. The answer that means the same as FEEBLE is **meager**.

(17)   The correct answer is: **C) breed – multiply, generate or reproduce.**

GENERATE – to make, produce or create. The answer that has the closest meaning to GENERATE is **breed.**

Test 3 Sentence Completion – Answers

(1)   The correct answer is: **D) reassured.**

Seeing the high score on my latest exam **reassured** me that I was doing well.

EXPLANATION: Options A, B and C all mean to discourage or take a toll. This is the opposite of "doing well."

(2)   The correct answer is: **A) stationery.**

We got the new **stationary** for our company and it filled me with pride to see my name on the letterhead.

Explanation: A and C are both forms of advertisements. C could be a possible option since letterhead is a business material, but it's a vague term. **Stationery** is a specific kind of material that letterheads are written on.

(3)   The correct answer is: **B) tropical.**

The **tropical** weather was warm and breezy as I walked along the shore.

Explanation: Tropical is the most fitting answer because tropical weather is usually in beach areas, with warm climates, and warm breezes that come in off the water. The Arctic is freezing cold weather, generally with snow; deserts are hot and dry and rainforests are hot, humid and muggy because of all the rain and heat.

(4)   The correct answer is: **C) so they went to bed without dessert.**

My children were being unruly at the restaurant, **so they went to bed without dessert**.

Explanation: The word **unruly** in the sentence means that the children were behaving badly. Options A, B and D all refer to rewarding their behavior. Since you are rewarded for good behavior and unruly means bad behavior, the children would get in trouble for not behaving so they had to go to bed early without dessert.

(5)   The correct answer is: **C) approximate.**

By feeling each object in the bag, the students were able to guess the **approximate** size and shape of the objects.

Explanation: Answers A, B and D mean that you know the size and shape usually because you can see it. Feeling the object means the students couldn't know the actual size or shape for sure and could only guess based on what they felt.

(6)   The correct answer is: **D) snow and ice made it impossible to drive anywhere.**

During the blizzard, the **snow and ice made it impossible to drive anywhere.**

(7)   The correct answer is: **A) my grandfather became too confused to make decisions.**

The judge assigned a guardian when **my grandfather became too confused to make decisions.**

(8)   The correct answer is: **B) eerie.**

The forest was dark and **eerie**, with bare tree branches, pointy shadows and odd noises as I walked home that night.

Explanation: Eerie is the best choice because A, C and D all mean pleasant, fun and bright. The sentence references things being dark and pointy, not bright or pleasant.

(9)   The correct answer is: **C) futile.**

My favorite movie quote is "Resistance is **futile.**"

Explanation: Options A, B and D mean interruptions or risings. C is the only option that fits. **Futile** means pointless, so to resist is pointless.

(10)   The correct answer is: **D) generate.**

The computers will **generate** new exams each week.

Explanation: Generate means to create, so the computer will create new exams each week.

(11)   The correct answer is: **A) source.**

I can't find the **source** of the burning smell.

(12)   The correct answer is: **B) cease.**

The judge issued a **cease** and desist order.

Explanation: The judge gave an order to stop something.

(13)   The correct answer is: **C) argument.**

My brother and I had a heated **argument** when he broke my favorite toy.

Explanation: Argument means fight or disagreement, so the brothers got into a fight when the toy was broken.

(14)   The correct answer is: **D) evaluate.**

This exam will help to **evaluate** us on a level field.

Explanation: Evaluate means to test or examine.

(15)   The correct answer is: **A) achievements.**

Making the Dean's List is one of the highest **achievements** you can attain at our school.

Explanation: Achievement means accomplishment. Making the Dean's List is a great accomplishment.

(16)   The correct answer is: **B) crave.**

My mother would **crave** anchovy pizza and ice cream each time she got pregnant.

Explanation: Crave means to have a strong urge for or want badly.

(17)   The correct answer is: **B) due.**

My history project was **due** on Friday.

Explanation: Due means to be ready on a specific date or time. **Do** means to act or make something happen. **Dew** is formed when the heat and cold of the ground and air mix and cause water to collect.

Test 3 Answers – Quantitative Reasoning

(1)   The correct answer is: **D) There are 6 houses that are gray.**

(2)   The correct answer is: **B) Average.**

(3)   The correct answer is: **B) Ensuring that the denominators are the same.**

(4)   The correct answer is: **D) 7 × 14**

(5)   The correct answer is: **B) Alisha works 5 out of 7 days of the week.**

(6)   The correct answer is: **C) There are 200 tickets left to be sold.**

(7)   The correct answer is: **C) Lisa needs to purchase 12 more sets of curtains.**

(8)   The correct answer is: **C) Milo can dive for 2 hours before he will need a fresh oxygen tank.**

(9)   The correct answer is: **B) Marissa's repairs will cost around $1,080.**

(10)   The correct answer is: **A) The total cost of the fishing cabin is $900.**

(11)   The correct answer is: **B) It will take Steven 4 hours to get to Morton.**

(12)   The correct answer is: **A) Megan had 3/8 of the pizza, Stacy had 2/8 of the pizza and Kelly had 3/8 of the pizza.**

(13)   The correct answer is: **D) Mark earned 75 cents on Saturday.**

(14)   The correct answer is: **C) A student will have read 84 pages by next Thursday.**

(15)   The correct answer is: **B) James needs to review 6 pages of study material each night.**

(16)   The correct answer is: **A) Every student has a 1 in 26 chance of guessing correctly, a ratio of 1:26.**

(17)   The correct answer is: **B) Anna collected between 20 and 30 stones.**

(18)   The correct answer is: **A) The platter contains 6/10 fruit and 4/10 veggies.**

(19)   The correct answer is: **D) The dogs walk 3 miles each day.**

(20)   The correct answer is: **C) Aaron swims 45 laps a week.**

(21)   The correct answer is: **A) There will be 48 pink rows on the blanket.**

(22)   The correct answer is: **D) Sheena's workforce is made up of around 62% men.**

(23)   The correct answer is: **C) Joseph and Josie were married in 1995.**

(24)   The correct answer is: **B) The average age of all five girls is 13 years old.**

(25)   The correct answer is: **A) The area of Mia's office is 648 sq. ft.**

(26)   The correct answer is: **D) 1/3 of his cars will be left out.**

(27)   The correct answer is: **A) 1/2.**

(28)   The correct answer is: **C) The hole for the window needs to be 44 inches wide.**

(29)   The correct answer is: **A) 75 psi.**

(30)   The correct answer is: **C) 80/20.**

(31)   The correct answer is: **B) There are four quarter horses and four palominos.**

(32)   The correct answer is: **A) There will be 264 softballs out on the field.**

(33)   The correct answer is: **A) There are 10 bar seats.**

(34)   The correct answer is: **D) Horton sat on the egg for 120 hours.**

(35)   The correct answer is: **B) Mia will need to make 48 muffins.**

(36)   The correct answer is: **A) The other team has 25% fewer players than Adam's team.**

(37)   The correct answer is: **A) The blue team scored 10 points in the first half and 33 points in the second half.**

(38)   The correct answer is: **A) 6 gallons of paint will need to be purchased to paint Alay's room.**

Test 3 Answers – Reading Comprehension

Test 3 Passage 1 – Answers

This passage is about scientists taking the first picture of a Black Hole.

(1)   The correct answer is. **C) An object of mass, packed tight, with strong gravity that doesn't let anything escape.**

QUESTION: What is a Black Hole?

EXPLANATION: The answer to this question can be found in lines 20-23: "Surprisingly, a Black Hole isn't a hole at all. It's an object that has so much mass stuffed into a small space that it creates a very powerful gravitational pull. It's so powerful, in fact, that not even light can escape it."

(2)   The correct answer is: **A) Sagittarius A* is located in the Milky Way Galaxy.**

QUESTION: What galaxy is Sagittarius A* located in?

EXPLANATION: The answer to this question can be found in line 13: "The first location, Sagittarius A*, is at the center of our Milky Way Galaxy."

(3)   The correct answer is: **D) M87* is located in the Gargantuan Galaxy.**

QUESTION: What galaxy is M87* located in?

EXPLANATION: The answer to this question can be found in line 15: "The second is M87*, which is in the Gargantuan Elliptical Galaxy."

(4)   The correct answer is: **C) They are hoping to take a real-time video of the black hole.**

QUESTION: What are they hoping to achieve with the next-generation EHT?

EXPLANATION: The answer to this question can be found in lines 26-27: "What they are calling the next generation EHT or ngEHT will allow them to take real-time videos of the black holes rather than the photographs they are getting now."

(5)   The correct answer is: **B) Sagittarius A* is 26,000 light-years away.**

QUESTION: How many light-years away is the black hole Sagittarius A*?

EXPLANATION: The answer to this question can be found in lines 13-14: "The first location, Sagittarius A*, is at the center of our Milky Way Galaxy. It is 26,000 light-years from Earth."

Test 3 Passage 2 – Answers

This passage is about the invention of the internet.

(1)   The correct answer is: **C) Sir Tim Berners-Lee is from London, England.**

QUESTION: Where is Sir Tim Berners-Lee from?

EXPLANATION: The answer to this question can be found in line 11: "Sir Tim Berners-Lee is an English engineer and computer scientist from London, England."

(2)   The correct answer is: **B) The three formats still used today that Tim created are HTML, URL and HTTP.**

QUESTION: What three formats did Tim create for the internet that we still use now?

EXPLANATION: The answer to this question can be found in lines 24-26: "By October he had made huge strides in his programming, creating three core formats that we still use today. Those programs are HTML, URI (also called URL) and HTTP."

(3)   The correct answer is: **A) When creating the World Wide Web, Tim used Steve Jobs' NeXT computer.**

QUESTION: What early Steve Jobs creation did Tim use when creating the World Wide Web?

EXPLANATION: The answer to this question can be found in line 23: "Tim used a NeXT computer, created by Steve Jobs, to start his project in September 1990."

(4)   The correct answer is: **A) Tim could see that there was a disconnect for scientists sharing information and communicating.**

QUESTION: What problem did Tim see while working for CERN that prompted him to create the internet?

EXPLANATION: The answer to this question can be found in lines 14, 18 and 19: "Tim took a job as a software engineer for a company called CERN ... Tim noticed a problem for these scientists though. There was a huge problem communicating and sharing information with so much distance."

(5)   The correct answer is: **B) They collaborated to make the internet available to everyone without charge or permission.**

QUESTION: What agreement did Tim and others collaborate with CERN on?

EXPLANATION: The answer to this question can be found in lines 31-33: "Seeing the true potential of his creation and its possibilities, Tim and others approached CERN about making the base coding available to everyone, without charge or permission, for the rest of the existence of the World Wide Web."

Test 3 Passage 3 – Answers

This passage is a poem about the night, the moon and the stars.

(1)   The correct answer is: **D) All of the above.**

QUESTION: What is the poem talking about?

EXPLANATION: The answer to this question can be logically concluded based on the descriptions throughout the poem such as lines 4 and 5 where it says, "High above me your glowing ball sits, casting down around me a glow." referring to the moon. In lines 3 and 6-8, the poem talks about the stars and constellations: "Either way your face will glow with dancing lights upon it ... Scorpio plays and Gemini dances, while Libra makes a happy home. The Big and Little Dippers play games of tag." Lines 12, 13 and 22 also provide evidence for the correct answer: "When the sun comes out to play, all my sky friends hide away ... We see the same moon, me and you."

(2)   The correct answer is: **B) Stars that make pictures.**

QUESTION: What are Scorpio, Gemini, Libra, the Little Dipper and Big Dipper?

EXPLANATION: The answer to this question can be logically concluded by the inferences made in the poem about their activities like playing, dancing, making a happy home and playing tag, mentioned in lines 6-8.

(3)   The correct answer is: **C) That when you are far apart, you feel together when you both see the moon.**

QUESTION: What does the line "We see the same moon, me and you," mean?

EXPLANATION: The answer to this question can be logically concluded based on the implications made in lines 16-22: "You chase away the dark, dark night. You are my perfect nightlight, watching over me from high above. I know that I am always loved. For when I'm in bed at night, looking up at such a sight, my dad abroad can look up too. We see the same moon, me and you."

(4)   The correct answer is: **C) The glowing ball in the poem is the moon.**

QUESTION: What is the "glowing ball" in the poem?

EXPLANATION: The answer to this question can be logically concluded based on lines 4, 5, 12, 13, 15, 16, and 22. "High above me, your glowing ball sits, casting down around me a glow ... When the sun comes out to play, all my sky friends hide away ... When you are here, I do not fear. You chase away the dark, dark night ... We see the same moon, me and you."

(5)   The correct answer is: **A) Cotton balls in the poem refer to the clouds.**

QUESTION: What do "cotton balls" represent in the poem?

EXPLANATION: The answer is a logical conclusion based on the information in the poem about the moon and stars in lines 9-11. "From time to time, cotton balls float by, hiding you from my sight when they do, and sometimes your glowing ball hides too."

Test 3 Passage 4 – Answers

This passage is about the Smithsonian Institute's National Zoo.

(1)   The correct answer is: **A) The National Zoo was founded in 1889.**

QUESTION: When was the National Zoo founded?

EXPLANATION: The answer to this question can be found in line 1: "The Smithsonian National Zoo was founded in 1889."

(2)   The correct answer is: **A) The first permanent animal enclosure was the Great Ape House.**

QUESTION: What was the first animal enclosure to find a permanent home at the zoo?

EXPLANATION: The answer to this question can be found in lines 4-6: "The primate enclosure found its permanent residents at the National Zoo on April 15, 1981. Gorillas, apes, orangutans, lemurs and monkeys are some of the animals that make their home here in the Great Ape House."

(3)   The correct answer is: **D) The Kids' Farm was added on June 12, 2004.**

QUESTION: What exhibit was added on June 12, 2004?

EXPLANATION: The answer to this question can be found in line 12: "On June 12, 2004, the Kids' Farm was added."

(4)   The correct answer is: **A) The 75 Years of Fighting Wildfires exhibit is on display on May 22nd.**

QUESTION: What special exhibit is currently on display on May 22nd?

EXPLANATION: The answer to this question can be found in lines 18-19: "The zoo is also running a Celebrate Smokey: 75 Years of Fighting Wildfires special exhibit on May 22, 2020."

(5)   The correct answer is: **D) The National Zoo is located in Rock Creek Park.**

QUESTION: Where is the National Zoo located?

EXPLANATION: The answer to this question can be found in line 2: "The zoo is located in Rock Creek Park in Washington, D.C."

Test 3 Passage 5 – Answers

This passage is about the Great Lakes of North America, which are located around the state of Michigan and between the U.S. and Canadian borders.

(1)   The correct answer is: **B) The Great Lakes are made up of five lakes.**

QUESTION: How many lakes make up the Great Lakes?

EXPLANATION: The answer can be found in lines 3, 4 and 7 of this passage: "The Great Lakes are made up of Lake Superior, Lake Michigan, Lake Huron, Lake Erie and Lake Ontario … These five lakes make up what is known as the Great Lakes Waterway…"

(2)   The correct answer is: **C) Lake Michigan is the only lake that is wholly in the United States.**

QUESTION: Which Great Lake is the only one wholly in the United States?

EXPLANATION: The answer to this question can be found in lines 5-6: "Lake Michigan is the only one of the Great Lakes that is located completely in the United States, while the others border both the United States and Canada."

(3)   The correct answer is: **B) The locks allow ships to move between the Great Lakes and the ocean.**

QUESTION: What allows ships to move between the Great Lakes and the Ocean?

EXPLANATION: The answer to this question can be found in lines 12-14: "The Great Lakes meet the Atlantic Ocean through the Saint Lawrence Seaway. Ships must be small enough to move through the lock of the Saint Lawrence Seaway in order to access the Great Lakes."

(4)   The correct answer is: **C) The Great Lakes also border the country of Canada.**

QUESTION: What country do the Great Lakes border in addition to the U.S.?

EXPLANATION: The answer to this question can be found in line 6: "…while the others border both the United States and Canada."

(5)   The correct answer is: **A) The Great Lakes make up 21 percent of the Earth's freshwater surface.**

QUESTION: What percentage of freshwater surface do the Great Lakes make up on Earth?

EXPLANATION: The answer to this question can be found in lines 7-8: "These five lakes make up what is known as the Great Lakes Waterway and by combined volume make up 21 percent of the world's surface freshwater."

Test 3 Mathematics Achievement

(1)   The correct answer is: **D) 25% of the cookies are M&M or turtle cookies.**

EXPLANATION: If there are 100 cookies total, then each cookie is 1%. There are 15 turtle cookies and 10 M&M cookies. 15 + 10 = 25. Therefore, 25% of the cookies are M&M or turtle cookies.

(2)   The correct answer is: **D) Chris drives 81 miles each workweek.**

EXPLANATION: If Chris drives 6 miles to work and 6 miles back home, then 6 + 6 = 12, so Chris drives 12 miles a day to and from work. Three nights a week his trip home is extended by 7 miles, so 12 + 7 = 19; Chris drives 19 miles on the days he goes to the store. If Chris goes to the store three of the five workdays (19 × 3 = 57 or 19 + 19 + 19 = 57), he drives 19 miles a day three days a week, and 12 miles a day two days a week, since all his driving is done on the 5 workdays each week. 19 × 3 = 57 + 24 = 81. Chris drives 81 miles in a five-day workweek.

(3)   The correct answer is: **B) The GCF of 16, 32 and 64 is 16.**

(4)   The correct answer is: **A) The square root of forty-nine.**

(5)   The correct answer is: **A) 12 is the square root of 144.**

EXPLANATION: The square root of a number must multiply by itself to give that number. Twelve multiplied by itself is 144. (12 × 12 = 144).

(6)   The correct answer is: **B) A = width × length.**

(7)   The correct answer is: **A) 7 is the square root of 49.**

(8)   The correct answer is: **B) Twenty-seven million, four hundred fifty-six thousand, nine-hundred eighty-seven.**

(9)   The correct answer is: **D) $5,229.62.**

(10)   The correct answer is: **A) Tens.**

EXPLANATION: The place values move from the right to the left on the positive side of the decimal place. Those places are ones, tens, hundreds, thousands, ten thousands, hundred thousands, millions, ten millions, hundred millions and so on. Therefore, the place value of the number 6 is the tens place.

(11)   The correct answer is: **B) $20\frac{2}{3}$.**

EXPLANATION: Twenty is a whole number and written first. Two-thirds is a fraction represented by two over three or $\frac{2}{3}$.

(12)   The correct answer is: **A) Tenths.**

(13)   The correct answer is: **C) $\frac{60}{100}$**

EXPLANATION: Percentages are proportions given out of 100. Therefore, 60% would be 60/100 as a fraction.

(14)   The correct answer is: **B) Each player has a 12.5% chance of winning.**

EXPLANATION: Alan and 7 friends are playing the game. Therefore, 8 people are playing Monopoly. A percentage is figured out of 100. To find the percentage of chance each player has at winning, divide 100 by the number of total players (8): $100 \div 8 = 12.5$.

(15)   The correct answer is: **A) >.**

(16)   The correct answer is: **C) 45 × 10 > 220 ÷ 2.**

EXPLANATION: 45 × 10 = 450; 220 ÷ 2 = 110. Out of A, B, C and D, only the answer C correctly expresses the word problem.

(17)   The correct answer is: **A) 6 + 4 + 6 = 16 miles.**

EXPLANATION: The equation that correctly expresses the word problem is 6 miles + 4 miles + 6 miles = 16. So Marissa runs 16 miles each day.

(18)   The correct answer is: **A) 114.**

EXPLANATION: Using the values provided, the equation becomes (49 ÷ 7) − (12 ÷ 3) + (37 × 3) = ? Solve each calculation in brackets first: (49 ÷ 7) = 7, (12 ÷ 3) = 4, and (37 × 3) = 111. Use the solutions to those calculations to solve the equation 7 − 4 + 111. 7 − 4 = 3 + 111 = 114.

(19)   The correct answer is: **B) c = 4.**

EXPLANATION: To solve for the unknown c, you need to work the problem backward. 105 − 9 = 96 and 96 ÷ 24 = 4. Therefore, c = 4. Then check your answer by solving the equation 24 × 4 + 9 = ? to ensure the answer comes out to 105: 24 × 4 = 96. 96 + 9 = 105. Working the problem after you have found c is important to ensure you have the correct answer.

(20)   The correct answer is: **B) There are 13 sixth graders to every 12 fifth graders or a 13:12 ratio.**

EXPLANATION: To determine the ratio, first find the GCF of 240 and 260. The GCF of 240 and 260 is 20. Divide each of the numbers by 20. 240 ÷ 20 = 12, and 260 ÷ 20 = 13. The two numbers you have arrived at (12 and 13) can be used to express the ratio in lowest terms. Therefore, there are 12 fifth graders to every 13 sixth graders. The question specifically asks what the ratio of sixth graders to fifth graders is: 13:12. This means that for every 13 sixth grade students there are 12 fifth graders.

(21)   The correct answer is: **C) 1,550,000,000.**

EXPLANATION: The ten millions place is the eighth numerical place in a positive number from right to left. When you round, you use the number to the right to determine if you round up or down. Zero through four rounds down and five through nine rounds up. In the number 1,547,698,321 the number 4 is in the ten millions place. Beside it is the number 7, so you round the 4 up to 5 and the numbers to the right will all become zero because you are rounding to the nearest ten million. So the number becomes 1,550,000,000.

(22)   The correct answer is: **C) The GCF of 18, 36 and 63 is 9.**

EXPLANATION: The greatest number that 18, 36 and 63 can all be divided by exactly is 9.

(23)   The correct answer is: **D) $252.15**

EXPLANATION: $252 is the whole dollar amount. When expressing the cents in a word problem with money, your decimal point is represented by the word **and**. Therefore, the correct numerical expression for the word problem is $252.15.

(24)   The correct answer is: **C) $a = 16$.**

EXPLANATION: To solve for a, divide 64 by 4: $64 \div 4 = 16$. To ensure that your answer is correct, solve the equation using 16 as a: $64 \div 16 = 4$.

(25)   The correct answer is: **A) 70,000,000,000 + 400,000,000 + 50,000,000 + 900,000 + 80,000 + 7,000 + 600 + 20 + 5**

EXPLANATION: To write a number in expanded form, write each place value out, with an addition sign between each. $70{,}000{,}000{,}000 + 400{,}000{,}000 + 50{,}000{,}000 + 900{,}000 + 80{,}000 + 7{,}000 + 600 + 20 + 5 = 70{,}450{,}987{,}625$

(26)   The correct answer is: **C) Alan is 7 feet 3 inches tall, Scott is 6 feet 9 inches tall and Dan is seven feet tall.**

EXPLANATION: The question asks you to calculate the height of the men on the basketball team. You are given Travis' height of 6 feet 4 inches. Alan is 6 inches taller than Scott (Alan = Scott + 6 inches); Scott is 3 inches shorter than Dan (Scott = Dan − 3 inches) and Dan is 8 inches taller than Travis (Dan = Travis + 8 inches).

Using Travis' height to start, since the value is already given, work out the problem. Travis is 6 foot 4 inches, Dan is 8 inches taller than Travis. 6 foot 4 inches + 8 inches = 6 foot 12 inches (12 inches = 1 foot) so 6 + 1 = 7. Dan is 7 feet tall. Scott is 3 inches shorter than Dan. 7 feet − 3 inches = 6 feet 9 inches. Scott is 6 feet 9 inches tall. Alan is 6 inches taller than Scott. 6 feet 9 inches + 6 inches = 6 feet 15 inches = 7 feet 3 inches. So Alan is 7'3" tall, Scott is 6'9" tall, Dan is 7' tall and Travis is 6'4" tall.

(27)   The correct answer is: **C) 42% of Kate's guests are male.**

EXPLANATION: There are 12 goody bags: 7 for female guests and 5 for male guests. Percentages are out of 100. $100 \div 12 = 8.3$, so each guest is represented by 8.3% of the whole party. To find the percentage of male guests, multiply 8.3 by the number of male guests ($8.3 \times 5 = 41.5$). Round 41.5 to the nearest whole number to give 42. Therefore, male guests make up 42% of the party.

(28)   The correct answer is: **C) 27 wildflower arrangements.**

EXPLANATION: To solve this word problem, take the information you're given and use it to find the missing number. Melissa made a total of 100 arrangements. 100 arrangements – 36 rose arrangements – 25 carnation arrangements – 12 daisy arrangements (100 – 36 – 25 – 12 = 27). 27 arrangements are wildflowers.

(29)   The correct answer is: **B)** a = **12.**

EXPLANATION: To solve for a, you will work the problem with the information you have to solve for a. Start with the numbers in brackets (53 + 86) = 139. Take the value of the equation (1,669) and divide it by the total of the numbers in brackets (139); therefore, 1,669 ÷ 139 = 12. The number 12 is the value of a, a = 12.

(30)   The correct answer is: **C) 1,171.72**

EXPLANATION: The calculation 0.1876 + 1.5876 + 1,157.366 + 12.58 totals 1,171.7212. The problem asks for the total to be rounded to the nearest hundredth. The hundredths place is the second place value to the right of the decimal point. The number 2 is in the hundredths place and the number 2 is in the ten-thousandths place. The number 1 is the number that helps you to know if you should round up or down. Numbers 1 through 4 round down. Therefore, 1,171.7212 is rounded down to 1,171.72.

Test 4: Verbal Reasoning

In the Verbal Reasoning section of this practice test, you will find practice questions that require you to do one of two things. You will either choose the **synonym** that means the same or similar thing to the **CAPITALIZED** word beside each numbered question, or you will be asked to choose from the multiple-choice answers to select the word or phrase that most logically **completes the sentence** you're given.

Synonym Directions: For the following practice test questions, read the **CAPITALIZED** word carefully. Choose the multiple-choice answer that means the same or close to the same as the **CAPITALIZED** word.

(1)   HAZY

(A)   clear

(B)   distinct

(C)   unencumbered

(D)   obscured

(2)   INEPT

(A)   incompetent

(B)   useful

(C)   hopeful

(D)   hearty

(3)   JUBILATION

(A)   unhappy

(B)   euphoria

(C)   depression

(D)   anticlimactic

(4) LEEWAY

(A) servitude

(B) impractical

(C) flexibility

(D) suffocation

(5) MISCHIEF

(A) obedient

(B) behaved

(C) harmless

(D) wayward

(6) NONCHALANT

(A) flippant

(B) formal

(C) concerned

(D) passionate

(7) OMNISCIENT

(A) smart aleck

(B) infinite

(C) immature

(D) unintelligent

(8) PETRIFY

(A) sedate

(B) resonate

(C) fossilize

(D) liquefy

(9)   RELUCTANT

(A)   enthusiastic

(B)   loving

(C)   willing

(D)   averse

(10)   SLUGGISH

(A)   lethargic

(B)   enthusiastic

(C)   lively

(D)   breakneck

(11)   TERRAIN

(A)   skyline

(B)   topography

(C)   vegetation

(D)   lustrous

(12)   URBAN

(A)   rural

(B)   country

(C)   metropolitan

(D)   suburban

(13)   VIVID

(A)   dull

(B)   muted

(C)   cloudy

(D)   vibrant

(14)   PROTAGONIST

(A)   hero

(B)   villain

(C)   damsel

(D)   sidekick

(15)   ORIGINATE

(A)   conclusion

(B)   initiate

(C)   omega

(D)   verdict

(16)   CONSPICUOUS

(A)   inconspicuous

(B)   muted

(C)   striking

(D)   hidden

(17)   DOMINATE

(A)   wallflower

(B)   dedicate

(C)   follow

(D)   govern

Sentence Completion Directions: For the following practice test questions, choose the answer that logically completes each sentence. Then read the question to yourself again with the answer you've chosen to ensure that it still makes sense to you, before moving on to the next one.

Test 4 Sentence Completion

(1)   My paper chain decorations hanging from the tree began to ____ in the rain.

(A)   float

(B)   glisten

(C)   disintegrate

(D)   combust

(2)   Diving on the coral reef was like ____ myself into a whole new world.

(A)   disappearing

(B)   contaminating

(C)   reflecting

(D)   immersing

(3)   By the time I left work, it was getting dark and I didn't want to ____.

(A)   linger

(B)   persist

(C)   endure

(D)   abide

(4)   I joined the huddle as we decided ____.

(A)   the next play to win the game.

(B)   the most outrageous thing to do.

(C)   who had the best score.

(D)   the least likely win.

(5)   The best ____ home is through the park, past the bakery and over the creek.

(A)   trail

(B)   road

(C)   route

(D)   story

(6)   It's time to ____ this horrible place and find a more suitable home.

(A)   remain

(B)   linger

(C)   bide

(D)   vacate

(7)   Water is ____ to the survival of the human body.

(A)   shoddy

(B)   vital

(C)   banal

(D)   tawdry

(8)   The dress I have chosen for the governor's arrival will ____ between the colors of blue and gold.

(A)   consistent

(B)   auxiliary

(C)   alternate

(D)   jumble

(9)   Their banquet for the jubilee will be full of delicious ____.

(A)   food and treats.

(B)   song and dance.

(C)   music and merriment.

(D)   gowns and riches.

(10)   The strength of your ____ goes a long way to show the kind of person you are.

(A)   pride

(B)   intellect

(C)   brutality

(D)   character

(11)   The ____ needs to be signed in order to close on the purchase of the new house.

(A)   document

(B)   telegraph

(C)   investment

(D)   lease

(12)   The world will ____ if we allow hatred to tear us apart.

(A)   sore

(B)   perish

(C)   elevate

(D)   ascend

(13)   I want to create a/an ____ for my relaxation and enjoyment.

(A)   aviary

(B)   corral

(C)   oasis

(D)   penitentiary

(14)   My father's accountant is a loathsome, ____ little man who often makes messes of things.

(A)   pleasant

(B)   competent

(C)   divine

(D)   inept

(15)   My best friend David is my ____ companion and only confidant.

(A)   constant

(B)   superior

(C)   felonious

(D)   trepidations

(16)   A wolf pup appeared on our doorstep last year. Surprisingly, he has become quite ____.

(A)   ferocious

(B)   domesticated

(C)   sullen

(D)   deviant

(17)   I had a wonderful time at Grandpa's house and ____.

(A)   I was sorry to have to say buy.

(B)   I was sorry to have to say by.

(C)   I was sorry to have to say bye.

(D)   None of the above.

Test 4: Quantitative Reasoning

Directions: In this section, you will find a variety of questions that test your quantitative reasoning skills. The questions in this section will involve a variety of mathematical skills including mathematical operations, measurements, probability, logical reasoning and more. You will be provided with additional information such as graphs or shapes if they are needed for a specific question.

Read each of the questions and answers carefully. If unsure, consider what information is provided with each possible answer. Eliminate the answers you know don't fit until you reach the most logical answer.

(1)   The block around our house measures 4 miles. Sam runs around the block twice a day. How do you figure out how many blocks Sam runs in six days?

(A)   (4 + 2) 6 = number of blocks run in six days

(B)   (4 × 2) + 6 = number of blocks run in six days

(C)   (4 × 2) 6 = number of blocks run in six days

(D)   4 (2) + (4) 6 = number of blocks run in six days

(2)   Nate has four packages to mail. Packages cost 20 cents (e) a pound. Package (A) is 4 pounds, package (B) is 9 pounds, package (C) is 6 pounds and the total cost (T) to send the packages was $4.60. What word problem best explains the equation you would use to figure out the weight of the package (D)?

(A)   Add the weights of packages A, B and C together. Divide the total cost by the total pounds of the packages you have. Multiply that total by 20 to get the weight of package D.

(B)   Divide the total cost by 20 cents ($0.20) to find out the total weight of the packages sent. Then take the total weight in pounds and subtract the weight of packages A, B and C. This will give you the weight of package D by elimination.

(C)   Add packages A, B and C together to get their combined weight. Take the cost of four dollars and sixty cents and subtract the total weight of the three packages. This will be the cost of package D.

(D)   Multiply 20 cents by the weight of each package separately. That will tell you how much each package costs to ship. Subtract the cost of each package from the total shipping cost. This will give you the cost of package D.

(3)   Anna has to feed nine baby elephants so she is preparing bottles in the kitchen. Which unit of measurement is she most likely to use to measure the formula for their giant bottles?

(A)   Ounces

(B)   Gallons

(C)   Cups

(D)   Liters

(4)   Based on the chart, there are a total of 100 students in Carmen's grade. What transportation option is used least by the students in her grade?

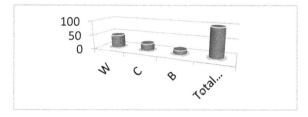

(A)   Column W – students who walk

(B)   Column C – students who get car rides

(C)   Column B – students who take the bus

(D)   The same number of students use each method of transportation.

(5)   Aaron is building an A-frame house on the lake. What is the most likely shape of an A-frame house?

(A)   Aaron's A-frame house on the lake is shaped like an oval.

(B)   Aaron's A-frame house on the lake is shaped like a diamond.

(C)   Aaron's A-frame house on the lake is shaped like a triangle.

(D)   Aaron's A-frame house on the lake is shaped like a circle.

(6)   In science class, Tyler is measuring out liquids for his science experiment. What unit of measurement would he use to do this?

(A)   Miles

(B)   Grams

(C)   Fluid ounces

(D)   Cups

(7)   Which equation properly expresses nine to the third power is 729?

(A) $9^3 = 729$

(B) $9 \times 3 = 729$

(C) $729 = \pi r^2$

(D) $9\sqrt[3]{729}$

(8)   What is the mean of a set of numbers?

(A)   The total of a set of numbers.

(B)   The number that occurs most often.

(C)   The middle of a set of numbers.

(D)   The average of a set of numbers.

(9)   If the sum of Becky and Trish's age is 56 and the girls are the same age, how old are the girls?

(A)   Becky and Trish are 28 years old.

(B)   Becky and Trish are 29 years old.

(C)   Becky and Trish are 27 years old.

(D)   Becky and Trish are 26 years old.

(10)   What place value does the digit 8 hold in 976,823,654?

(A)   Hundred thousandths

(B)   Hundreds

(C)   Ten thousands

(D)   Hundred thousands

(11) $96\frac{6}{12}$, is known as what type of number?

(A) Numerator

(B) Fraction

(C) Mixed number

(D) Exponent

(12) A given number to the third power is known as____?

(A) The perfect square

(B) Cubed

(C) Squared

(D) To the fourth power

(13) There are 3 turtles in the turtle race. Turtle A is moving at 1 foot per minute, Turtle B is moving 12 inches per minute and Turtle C is moving at 30.48 centimeters per minute. Which turtle is moving the fastest?

(A) All three of the turtles are moving a foot per minute.

(B) Turtle C is moving the fastest.

(C) Turtle A is moving the fastest.

(D) Turtle A and Turtle C are moving the fastest.

(14)   On a number line, which of the following numbers is the farthest from the number 1?

(A)   -20

(B)   20

(C)   0

(D)   15

(15)   If $\frac{1}{4}$ of supplies are on back-order, what percentage are you waiting for?

(A)   35% of your supply order is on back-order.

(B)   40% of your supply order is on back-order.

(C)   60% of your supply order is on back-order.

(D)   25% of your supply order is on back-order.

(16)   What is the GCF of 3, 9, 12 and 18?

(A)   The GCF of 3, 9, 12 and 18 is 18.

(B)   The GCF of 3, 9, 12 and 18 is 9.

(C)   The GCF of 3, 9, 12 and 18 is 3.

(D)   The GCF of 3, 9, 12 and 18 is 1.

(17)   What is the LCM of 12, 24, 36 and 48?

(A)   The LCM of 12, 24, 36 and 48 is 12.

(B)   The LCM of 12, 24, 36 and 48 is 112.

(C)   The LCM of 12, 24, 36 and 48 is 6.

(D)   The LCM of 12, 24, 36 and 48 is 144.

(18)   What is the LCM of 100, 400 and 800?

(A)   The LCM of 100, 400 and 800 is 800.

(B)   The LCM of 100, 400 and 800 is 400.

(C)   The LCM of 100, 400 and 800 is 100.

(D)   The LCM of 100, 400 and 800 is 200.

(19)   What are the prime factors of 111 in lowest terms?

(A)   The factors of 111 are 11 and 10.

(B)   The factors of 111 are 11 and 2.

(C)   The factors of 111 are 36 and 3.

(D)   The factors of 111 are 37 and 3.

(20)   Which of the given numbers is a prime number?

(A)   190

(B)   193

(C)   194

(D)   196

(21)   Myles is driving to Harrison, 4 hours away. If Harrison is 54 miles away, approximately how many miles does Myles drive per hour if you round to the nearest whole number?

(A)   Myles drives approximately 12 miles per hour.

(B)   Myles drives approximately 13 miles per hour.

(C)   Myles drives approximately 14 miles per hour.

(D)   Myles drives approximately 15 miles per hour.

(22)   Which of the given numbers is a multiple of 49?

(A)   980 is a multiple of 49.

(B)   990 is a multiple of 49.

(C)   940 is a multiple of 49.

(D)   920 is a multiple of 49.

(23)   What equation correctly represents twelve billionths?

(A) -12×10

(B) 10×12^9

(C) 12×10^9

(D) 12×10^{-9}

(24)   What is the LCD of $\frac{1}{2}, \frac{3}{4}, \frac{5}{6}$?

(A)   The LCD of this set of fractions is 10.

(B)   The LCD of this set of fractions is 12.

(C)   The LCD of this set of fractions is 14.

(D)   The LCD of this set of fractions is 16.

(25)   Micah buys inventory for his hardware store once a month. He keeps 4 of each item in stock and there are 17 items that need replenishing. If those items each have two left, how many items need to be ordered total?

(A)   Micah needs to order 68 items.

(B)   Micah needs to order 17 items.

(C)   Micah needs to order 74 items.

(D)   Micah needs to order 34 items.

(26)   If sales tax makes up 9% of city revenue, gift tax makes up 42% of city revenue, DMV fees make up 32% of city revenue, and educational taxes make up the rest, what percentage of the city's revenue is made from educational taxes?

(A)   Educational taxes make up 12% of the city's revenue.

(B)   Educational taxes make up 17% of the city's revenue.

(C)   Educational taxes make up 19% of the city's revenue.

(D)   Educational taxes make up 20% of the city's revenue.

(27)   Anna spent $54 at the stylist today. If her manicure was $10 and her pedicure was $12, and the rest was spend on a haircut, how much did her haircut cost?

(A)   Anna's haircut cost $25.

(B)   Anna's haircut cost $32.

(C)   Anna's haircut cost $40.

(D)   Anna's haircut cost $15.

(28)   Mavis wants to buy peaches for the peach cobbler she is making for a fundraiser. She plans to make 45 cobblers to sell in order to raise money for the animal shelter. Roughly how many peaches will she need if one bushel makes approximately 23 cobblers?

(A)   Mavis will need about 2 pints of peaches.

(B)   Mavis will need about 2 quarts of peaches.

(C)   Mavis will need about 2 bushels of peaches.

(D)   Mavis will need about 2 tons of peaches.

(29)   A recipe calls for one 8-ounce bag of chocolate chips for every batch of cookies. If Melissa is making 2 dozen batches of cookies, how many 8-ounce bags of chocolate chips will she need?

(A)   Melissa will need 8 bags of chocolate chips.

(B)   Melissa will need 12 bags of chocolate chips.

(C)   Melissa will need 16 bags of chocolate chips.

(D)   Melissa will need 24 bags of chocolate chips.

(30)   Each archer gets five arrows from the 10-meter line and five from the 15-meter line. How many chances does an archer get to score a bull's-eye from each position?

(A)   Each archer will have 1 chance to score a bull's-eye from each position.

(B)   Each archer will have 5 chances to score a bull's-eye from each position.

(C)   Each archer will have 10 chances to score a bull's-eye from each position.

(D)   Each archer will have 15 chances to score a bull's-eye from each position.

(31)   Which of the following word problems writes the inequality $x > 56$ correctly?

(A) x is greater than fifty-six.

(B) x is less than or equal to fifty-six.

(C)   The absolute value of x is fifty-six.

(D) x is less than fifty-six.

(32)   In $12\frac{6}{8}$, the number 12 is what?

(A)   The numerator

(B)   The denominator

(C)   A whole number

(D)   A mixed number

(33)   If the mural canvas is 12 feet high by 12 feet long, what is the shape of the mural?

(A)   The mural is most likely a rectangle.

(B)   The mural is most likely an oval.

(C)   The mural is most likely a triangle.

(D)   The mural is most likely a square.

(34)   Paul has a sofa that is 55 inches high and 42 inches wide. Paul's doorway needs to be at least how many feet wide for the sofa to fit through it?

(A)   The doorway needs to be at least 2 feet wide.

(B)   The doorway needs to be at least 3 feet wide.

(C)   The doorway needs to be at least 4 feet wide.

(D)   The doorway needs to be at least 5 feet wide.

(35)   Amy is 12 years younger than Lynne, Mary is four years older than Lynne and Debbie is six years older than Mary. If Amy is 36, how old are Lynne, Debbie and Mary?

(A)   Lynne is 48, Mary is 52 and Debbie is 58.

(B)   Lynne is 46, Mary is 50 and Debbie is 56.

(C)   Lynne is 42, Mary is 48 and Debbie is 54.

(D)   Lynne is 40, Mary is 44 and Debbie is 46.

(36)   If ski slope A is at a 30-degree incline, slope B is 30 degrees steeper than C and slope C is 10 degrees steeper than slope A, what is the degree of each of the slopes?

(A)   A is flat, B is 30 degrees and C is 10 degrees.

(B)   A is 30 degrees, B is 70 degrees and C is 40 degrees.

(C)   A is 30 degrees, B is 60 degrees and C is 70 degrees.

(D)   A is 30 degrees, B is flat and C is 40 degrees.

(37)   There are seven leaks in the barn roof. When it rains, Emily has to change the buckets under the three largest leaks every hour, the buckets under the medium leak every three hours and the buckets under the three small leaks every six hours. If she places the buckets at 8:00 p.m., what time will she need to change each of the buckets?

(A)   She'll have to change the large leak buckets at 9 p.m., the medium leak bucket at 11 p.m. and the small leak buckets at 2 a.m.

(B)   She'll have to change the large leak buckets at 9 p.m., the medium leak bucket at 12 a.m. and the small leak buckets at 6 a.m.

(C)   She'll have to change the large leak buckets at 8 p.m., the medium leak bucket at 10 p.m. and the small leak buckets at 4 a.m.

(D)   She'll have to change the large leak buckets at 9 p.m., the small leak buckets at 11 p.m. and the medium leak bucket at 2 a.m.

(38)   There are 6 different colors of jelly beans in the jar. If there are 300 jelly beans and there is the same number of each color, how many of each color are in the jar?

(A)   There are 25 of each color jelly bean in the jar.

(B)   There are 50 of each color jelly bean in the jar.

(C)   There are 75 of each color jelly bean in the jar.

(D)   There are 100 of each color jelly bean in the jar.

Test 4: Reading Comprehension

Directions: Read each passage carefully. Think about the main points, the feel of the passage, the information presented and anything that you feel the passage might be implying. When you are through reading each passage, carefully read through each multiple-choice answer you have been given. Use the information you gained from the passages and conclusions you have made about the passage to choose the correct answer for each.

Test 4 Passage 1 & Questions:

1.   On September 23, 1953, California senator
2.   Richard Nixon gave a televised speech to the American people.
3.   He had been announced two months earlier as Dwight D. Eisenhower's running mate.
4.   Shortly before his speech, a disgruntled nominee who had lost out to Nixon & Eisenhower
5.   for the presidential nomination ran to the press with a major story.
6.   The whole ordeal put Nixon's political career in peril.
7.   Richard Nixon left his West Coast tour and flew to L.A. to make his speech.
8.   Before the speech, his lawyers and accountants confirmed he had done nothing illegal
9.   and that no money was misused or unaccounted for.
10.   During his half-hour TV speech, Nixon did three things.
11.   He defended himself, saying he had never misused funds
12.   or given special favors to anyone, and he never would.
13.   His benefactors would never be given anything he wouldn't give to any other constituents.
14.   He continued by saying his government stipend only covered very specific things relating to
15.   his office and not his political career.
16.   He added that it would be morally wrong to charge the taxpayers for any of those expenses and
17.   said all the money in the fund had been used to pay for expenses in his political career.
18.   Then, he was transparent about his personal finances.
19.   He went after his opponents, saying they should also give a full accounting of their finances,
20.   as well as pointing out some shady things he felt some Democrats were doing.
21.   Nixon said he had done nothing wrong and he wasn't a quitter, so he wasn't giving up.
22.   He asked the American people to contact the Republican National Convention and tell them if
23.   he should or should not be on the ticket.
24.   He told the public that regardless of how things turned out, the one gift he wouldn't give back
25.   was a black and white dog his kids loved and called Checkers.
26.   Following the speech, the American people rallied behind Nixon.
27.   The RNC and local political offices received millions of calls and telegrams,

28. all of which supported Nixon and ensured his spot on the ticket as vice president.
29. The family dog, Checkers, gave Nixon's speech its name.

Directions: Using the passage above, answer each of the five questions that follow. Refer back to the passage to confirm your answer choices and refresh the details of your memory. The answers to all of the questions will either be in the passage or will require your opinion or point of view, so there is no outside information you need to know.

(1)   Why did Richard Nixon feel the need to give his Checkers speech?

(A)   Richard Nixon gave his Checkers speech to defend himself.

(B)   Richard Nixon gave his Checkers speech as proof that he had done nothing wrong.

(C)   Richard Nixon gave his Checkers speech to be transparent with the American people.

(D)   All of the above.

(2)   What role was Nixon trying to obtain at the time of the speech?

(A)   Richard Nixon was running for senator of California.

(B)   Richard Nixon was running for vice president of the United States.

(C)   Richard Nixon was running for president of the United States.

(D)   Richard Nixon was running for governor of Washington.

(3)   Following the speech, what was the reaction of the American people?

(A)   The American people supported Nixon.

(B)   The American people wanted Nixon to resign.

(C)   The American people supported his removal from the ticket.

(D)   The American people thought what he did was illegal.

(4)   Who was Checkers?

(A)   Checkers was Nixon's favorite car.

(B)   Checkers was the black and white family dog.

(C)   Checkers was the family tabby cat.

(D)   Checkers was the corruption in the government.

(5)   Where and when did Richard Nixon deliver his Checkers speech?

(A)   Richard Nixon gave his Checkers speech on August 1953, alongside Dwight D Eisenhower.

(B)   Richard Nixon gave his Checkers speech on the eve of the November 1953 elections.

(C)   Richard Nixon gave his Checkers speech on September 23, 1953, in L.A.

(D)   None of the above.

Test 4 Passage 2 & Questions:

1.   World War II is to date the deadliest international war in world history.
2.   Japan invaded China on September 19, 1931,
3.   though the landmark start of World War II was September 1, 1939,
4.   when Germany invaded Poland.
5.   World War II was a joint effort by Germany and the Soviet Union.
6.   Adolf Hitler and Joseph Stalin signed a non-aggression pact in August 1939.
7.   The idea was Hitler's. He wanted to grow a German race that would rival all others.
8.   He dubbed it the Aryan race and the war was meant to clear out the "trash"
9.   in order to make room for his Aryan race to grow and thrive.
10.   France and Great Britain, as allies of Poland,
11.   promised to support Poland with military forces if Germany invaded.
12.   So, when Germany invaded Poland from the west on September 1, 1939,
13.   France and Britain had to come to Poland's aid.
14.   Both countries declared war on Germany just two days later on September 3, 1939.
15.   The Soviet Union, in league with Germany, invaded Poland from the east.
16.   With Germany and the Soviet Union's joint attack, Poland fell on October 6, 1939.
17.   By the beginning of 1940, Germany and the Soviet Union, having occupied Poland,
18.   split control of Poland amongst themselves.
19.   WWII was split into two sides: the Allies and the Axis.
20.   The Axis was made up of Germany, Italy and Japan.
21.   The Allies were comprised of Great Britain, France and the United States.
22.   To the surprise of many, the Soviet Union also joined the Allies, after Germany broke its
23.   Non-aggression pact and invaded the Soviet Union.
24.   The United States only joined the war after the Japanese surprised the U.S.
25.   by bombing the Pearl Harbor Naval Base in Honolulu, Hawaii, on December 7, 1941.
26.   The bombing killed more than 2,300 service members.
27.   The attack shocked America and gave the American people a reason to support joining the war,
28.   which Congress did when it declared war on December 8, 1941, following the attack.
29.   The Allies gained significant ground in the war with the Battle of Midway and D-Day.

30. After land losses to Japan, it was decided that a land attack risked too many lives.
31. Instead, the decision was made to use the atomic bomb.
32. The A-bomb was only ever used twice.
33. The first time it was used was on August 6, 1945, in the bombing of Hiroshima.
34. The bomb was delivered by a B-29 bomber plane.
35. When the Japanese didn't surrender right away,
36. a second A bomb was used in the bombing of Nagasaki three days later on August 9, 1945.
37. The results were so devastating that the Japanese emperor surrendered over a radio broadcast
38. on August 15, 1945, finally ending World War II.
39. The officially surrender of Japan happened weeks later aboard the USS Missouri,
40. in Tokyo Bay on September 2, 1945.
41. To date, WWII is still the most deadly war internationally.

Directions: Using the passage above, answer each of the five questions that follow. Refer back to the passage to confirm your answer choices and refresh the details of your memory. The answers to all of the questions will either be in the passage or will require your opinion or point of view, so there is no outside information you need to know.

(1) What landmark event is considered to have started World War II?

(A) Japan's invasion of China is considered the catalyst that started World War II.

(B) Germany's invasion of the Soviet Union is considered the catalyst that started World War II.

(C) The Japanese bombing of Pearl Harbor is considered the catalyst that started World War II.

(D) The German invasion of Poland is considered the catalyst that started World War II.

(2) What were the two sides in WWII called?

(A) The two sides in World War II were Hitler and Stalin.

(B) The two sides in World War II were Great Britain and France.

(C) The two sides in World War II were the Allies and the Axis.

(D) The two sides in World War II were Hiroshima and Nagasaki.

(3)   What weapon was used to ultimately end WWII?

(A)   The B-29 bomber was used to ultimately end the war.

(B)   The atomic bomb was used to ultimately end the war.

(C)   The naval assault bomber was used to ultimately end the war.

(D)   The invasion bomber was used to ultimately end the war.

(4)   What major leader started WWI?

(A)   Joseph Stalin is considered to be the instigator of World War II.

(B)   President Truman is considered to be the instigator of World War II.

(C)   Adolf Hitler is considered to be the instigator of World War II.

(D)   The USS Missouri is considered to be the instigator of World War II.

(5)   Why did the Germans go to war?

(A)   The Soviet Union wanted more power.

(B)   Hitler wanted to make room to grow his Aryan race.

(C)   Japan wanted control of China.

(D)   The world needed an international war.

Test 4 Passage 3 & Questions:

1.   A building covered in bright red lacquer, trimmed in a striking white.

2.   A golden bell upon the steeple ringing out to signal the start of our day.

3.   Desks and chairs sit quietly as pupils file in evenly.

4.   Her heels click along the wood planks.

5.   The chalk dancing across the board ahead, clicking along the path it makes.

6.   A beautiful scroll of knowledge she writes.

7.   A skill we all hope to soon have right.

8.   She rings the brass bell upon her desk when it's time to take our lunch.

9.   With bellies full, we run and play until her handbell rings anew.

10.   In even rows, we file back in.

11.   We read, we write, we count to ten.

12.   Until the steeple bell chimes again.

13.   Time to find our way back home.

14.   To a warm embrace in our mother's home.

15.   To cozy beds where we close our day

16.   and we will start again another day.

Directions: Using the passage above, answer each of the five questions that follow. Refer back to the passage to confirm your answer choices and refresh the details of your memory. The answers to all of the questions will either be in the passage or will require your opinion or point of view, so there is no outside information you need to know.

(1)   What is the place the poem is talking about?

(A)   The poem is talking about a schoolhouse.

(B)   The poem is talking about a church.

(C)   The poem is talking about a house.

(D)   None of the above.

(2)   Who is the "she" and "her" in the poem referring to?

(A)   A mother

(B)   A teacher

(C)   A sister

(D)   A friend

(3)   What color is the bell in the steeple?

(A)   The bell in the steeple is red.

(B)   The bell in the steeple is white.

(C)   The bell in the steeple is gold.

(D)   The bell in the steeple is brass.

(4)   What color is the trim of the schoolhouse?

(A)   The trim on the schoolhouse is brass.

(B)   The trim on the schoolhouse is green.

(C)   The trim on the schoolhouse is red.

(D)   The trim on the schoolhouse is white.

(5)   Where do the pupils go when the bell rings at the end of the day?

(A)   At the end of the day, all of the pupils go to school.

(B)   At the end of the day, all of the pupils go home.

(C)   At the end of the day, all of the pupils go to recess.

(D)   At the end of the day, all of the pupils go to bed.

Test 4 Passage 4 & Questions:

1.   We stroll along the water's edge.
2.   Fallen trees and reeds they're home.
3.   The water shallow, the sun is hot.
4.   The perfect weather for their habitat.
5.   A hook concealed by a wormy treat.
6.   My bobber floats along lazily.
7.   A jerk from below sinks it deep.
8.   When the bobber disappears below,
9.   it's time to jerk my restless pole.
10.   Jerk it once and reel it fast.
11.   Soon I pull up a big fat bass.
12.   Slippery scales slide in my hand
13.   as I toss him in the bucket
14.   and save him for the frying pan.

Directions: Using the passage above, answer each of the five questions that follow. Refer back to the passage to confirm your answer choices and refresh the details of your memory. The answers to all of the questions will either be in the passage or will require your opinion or point of view, so there is no outside information you need to know.

(1)   What is the poem about?

(A)   The poem is about hiking.

(B)   The poem is about fishing.

(C)   The poem is about hunting.

(D)   The poem is about eating.

(2)   What conceals the hook in the poem?

(A)   In the poem, the hook is concealed by reeds.

(B)   In the poem, the hook is concealed by fallen trees.

(C)   In the poem, the hook is concealed by a wormy treat.

(D)   In the poem, the hook is concealed by the bucket.

(3)   What word describes the scales?

(A)   The scales on the fish are slippery.

(B)   The scales on the fish are lazy.

(C)   The scales on the fish are restless.

(D)   The scales on the fish are hot.

(4)   Where are they fishing?

(A)   The poem describes the fishing spot as shallow water.

(B)   The poem describes the fishing spot as at the shallow waters' edge.

(C)   The poem describes the fishing spot as shallow, near reeds and fallen trees.

(D)   All of the above.

(5)   What makes the perfect habitat?

(A)   The poem says the warm and shallow water make the perfect habitat.

(B)   The poem says the cool and breezy weather makes the perfect habitat.

(C)   The poem says the cold and deep water make the perfect habitat.

(D)   None of the above.

Test 4 Passage 5 & Questions:

1. Scotland is part of the United Kingdom now,
2. but when it was formed in the early middle ages it was its own country.
3. In 1603, King James VI of Scotland inherited England and Ireland.
4. After the death of Queen Elizabeth the I, who had no children,
5. and the dethroning and death of his mother, Mary Queen of Scots,
6. King James VI was the closest relative to inherit the throne,
7. thus becoming King James I of England and Ireland
8. in addition to his title of King James VI of Scotland.
9. That inheritance joined the three countries together.
10. King James VI joined the countries politically on May 1, 1707.
11. Despite the countries joining to become the New Kingdom of Great Britain,
12. Scotland has since and will continue to maintain its own identity.
13. Scotland has held onto many pre-union royal titles and symbols.
14. It also maintains its own legal, educational and religious systems,
15. among other self-defining characteristics.
16. Scotland maintains English, Scottish Gaelic, Scots and
17. British sign language as a common language throughout the country.
18. The country is separated by highlands and lowlands.
19. It borders the United Kingdom along the southeast.
20. It is surrounded by water on all other sides.
21. The Atlantic Ocean, the North Sea and the Irish Sea touch its borders.
22. Scotland has over 790 small islands as well.
23. While Scotland is well known for the city of Inverness
24. and the Loch Ness Monster, its capital city is actually Edinburgh.

Test 4 Passage 5 Questions:

Directions: Using the passage above, answer each of the five questions that follow. Refer back to the passage to confirm your answer choices and refresh the details of your memory. The answers to all of the questions will either be in the passage or will require your opinion or point of view, so there is no outside information you need to know.

(1)   When was Scotland formed?

(A)   Scotland was formed in 1707.

(B)   Scotland was formed in 1603.

(C)   Scotland was formed in the early middle ages.

(D)   Scotland was formed at the turn of the century.

(2)   Who joined Scotland with the United Kingdom?

(A)   Mary, Queen of Scots

(B)   King James VI

(C)   Queen Elizabeth I

(D)   None of the above.

(3)   What border do Great Britain and Scotland share?

(A)   Great Britain and Scotland share the southeastern Scottish border.

(B)   Great Britain and Scotland share the northeastern Scottish border.

(C)   Great Britain and Scotland share the northwestern Scottish border.

(D)   Great Britain and Scotland share the southwestern Scottish border.

(4)   What is the capital of Scotland?

(A)   The capital of Scotland is Inverness.

(B)   The capital of Scotland is London.

(C)   The capital of Scotland is Edinburgh.

(D)   The capital of Scotland is Ireland.

(5)   What borders Scotland on three sides?

(A)   Scotland is bordered on three sides by England.

(B)   Scotland is bordered on three sides by Ireland.

(C)   Scotland is bordered on three sides by the Atlantic Ocean.

(D)   Scotland is bordered on three sides by water.

Test 4 Mathematics Achievement

Directions: In this Mathematics Achievement practice test you will find a variety of mathematical questions that test your math skills as well as the information you have learned. The questions may include addition, subtraction, multiplication, and division, as well as square roots, geometry, measurements, probability, and overall problem-solving.

Read each question carefully. Then read each of the multiple-choice questions that follow. You will choose the multiple-choice answer that correctly solves each question, word problem, or equation. On your official exam, you will be allowed to use the space in your workbook or margins to solve the equations and choose the correct answer. With that in mind, you may use scratch paper to work out the equations in this study guide to reach the correct answers.

(1)   Mary had a jar of gumballs. The jar had 276 gumballs at the start. If Mary took one gumball out every day of the week and took two extra every Friday, how many gumballs would be left after 14 days if she started on a Monday?

(A)   Mary would have 264 gumballs left after 14 days.

(B)   Mary would have 260 gumballs left after 14 days.

(C)   Mary would have 258 gumballs left after 14 days.

(D)   Mary would have 256 gumballs left after 14 days.

(2)   Johan is flying from his home in Germany to his sisters' home in Italy, before flying to see his brother in America and finally returning home to Germany. The whole trip is 10,917 miles. If the trip from Germany to Italy is 650 miles and the trip from Italy to America is 5,369 miles, how many miles is the trip from America back home to Germany?

(A)   The trip from America to Germany is 4,898 miles.

(B)   The trip from America to Germany is 6,019 miles.

(C)   The trip from America to Germany is 10,267 miles.

(D)   The trip from America to Germany is 3,639 miles.

(3)   What is the √169?

(A)   The square root of 169 is 12.

(B)   The square root of 169 is 13.

(C)   The square root of 169 is 14.

(D)   The square root of 169 is 15.

(4)   What is the √289?

(A)   The square root of 289 is 16.

(B)   The square root of 289 is 17.

(C)   The square root of 289 is 18.

(D)   The square root of 289 is 19.

(5)   What is the area of this triangle?

(A)   The area of the triangle is 70 square inches.

(B)   The area of the triangle is 19 square inches.

(C)   The area of the triangle is 2.8 square inches.

(D)   The area of the triangle is 35 square inches.

(6)   What is the square root of 100?

(A)   The square root of 100 is 5.

(B)   The square root of 100 is 10.

(C)   The square root of 100 is 15.

(D)   The square root of 100 is 50.

(7)   Which of the following writes the number four hundred seven thousand six hundred ninety in the correct numerical form?

(A)   4,7690

(B)   4,700,600,090

(C)   407,690

(D)   400,070,690

(8)   Which answer correctly expresses one hundred twenty-five to the fifth power in numeric form?

(A) $100^{5\frac{2}{5}}$

(B) 100^5

(C) 125^5

(D) 5^{125}

(9)   Which of the following is the correct numerical form of twenty-one to the third power?

(A) 21^3

(B) $21^{\frac{1}{3}}$

(C) x_{y^2}

(D) $\frac{21}{3}$

(10)   Which word problem correctly expresses five hundred million, six hundred fifty-two thousand, eight hundred and five tenths?

(A)   500,652,800.50

(B)   500 + 652 + 8000 + 50

(C)   500,652,850

(D)   500,652,800,050

(11)   What is the GCF of 120, 160 and 220?

(A)   The GCF of 120, 160 and 220 is 10.

(B)   The GCF of 120, 160 and 220 is 30.

(C)   The GCF of 120, 160 and 220 is 20.

(D)   The GCF of 120, 160 and 220 is 60.

(12)   In the number five hundred sixty-two million, four hundred eight thousand, and seventy cents, what place value does the number six hold?

(A)   Ten thousandths

(B)   Ten millions

(C)   Thousands

(D)   Thousandths

(13) If 42% of students are in art class, 13% of students are in theater, 17% of students are in choir and the rest are in pottery class, what percent of students are in pottery class?

(A) 18% of students are in pottery class.

(B) 26% of students are in pottery class.

(C) 16% of students are in pottery class.

(D) 28% of students are in pottery class.

(14) Mike and Audrey are preparing 25 goody bags for the party on Saturday. Twenty people have sent their RSVP for the party. What percentage of those invited haven't sent an RSVP yet?

(A) 20% haven't RSVP'd for the party yet.

(B) 40% haven't RSVP'd for the party yet.

(C) 60% haven't RSVP'd for the party yet.

(D) 80% haven't RSVP'd for the party yet.

(15) Which of the following statements show four plus five is greater than four minus five?

(A) $4 + 9 > |4 - 5|$

(B) $4 + 5 > 4 - 5$

(C) $4 + 5 < 4 - 5$

(D) $4 + 5 = 4 - 5$

(16)   Which of the following statements show four multiplied by twelve is less than or equal to twelve multiplied by four?

(A) $4 \times 12 \geq 12 \times 4$

(B) $4 \times 12 < 12 \times 4$

(C) $4 \times 12 \leq 12 \times 4$

(D) $4 \times 12 > 12 \times 4$

(17)   Sarah runs twice a week for 6 miles and three times a week for 8 miles. How many miles does Sarah run in a week?

(A)   Sarah runs 36 miles each week.

(B)   Sarah runs 240 miles each week.

(C)   Sarah runs 70 miles each week.

(D)   Sarah runs 34 miles each week.

(18)   Solve for x: $11x + 13 = 112$

(A) $x = 3$

(B) $x = 9$

(C) $x = 6$

(D) $x = 12$

(19)   Using $a = 12$, $b = 49$, and $c = 37$, find the value of: $b - a + c = $ ___?

(A)   74

(B)   47

(C)   34

(D)   12

(20)   Lucy went out for lunch at her favorite restaurant today. She spent $54.54 on her meal. If she gives her waiter Kevin a 20% tip, how much will her bill be?

(A)   Lucy's total bill for lunch with Kevin's 20% tip will be $65.45.

(B)   Lucy's total bill for lunch with Kevin's 20% tip will be $59.99.

(C)   Lucy's total bill for lunch with Kevin's 20% tip will be $68.18.

(D)   Lucy's total bill for lunch with Kevin's 20% tip will be $62.84.

(21)   Round the number 4,598,632 to the nearest thousand.

(A)   4,598,000

(B)   4,599,000

(C)   4,597,000

(D)   4,500,00

(22)   Write 304,689,987 in expanded form.

(A)   300,000,000 + 4,000,000 + 600,000 + 80,000 + 9,000 + 900 + 80 + 7

(B)   304,000,000 + 689,000 + 987

(C)   34,689,987

(D)   300 + 689 +987

(23)   Calculate: 1,598,147 + 69,248 + 3,997 = ?

(A)   1,667,395

(B)   73,245

(C)   1,671,392

(D)   1,602,144

(24)   Calculate: $14 \div 7 \, (6 \times 6) + 42 = ?$

(A)   31,752

(B)   81

(C)   114

(D)   1,141

(25)   Which answer correctly expresses 80,000,000 + 7,000,000 + 1,000 in standard form?

(A)   80,701,000

(B)   80,007,001,000

(C)   807,100

(D)   87,001,000

(26) One million, seven hundred fifty-six thousand, twenty. What place value does the seven hold?

(A) Millions

(B) Hundred thousands

(C) Thousands

(D) Ten millions

(27) Kaden and Dominic are running a marathon at the end of the month. The boys run six miles a day, six days a week, for four weeks. How many miles do the boys run altogether?

(A) The boys run a total of 148 miles.

(B) The boys run a total of 40 miles.

(C) The boys run a total of 144 miles.

(D) The boys run a total of 48 miles.

(28) Mark's body shop repaired four vehicles this week and did two oil changes. Each oil change was $42.50. The blue car was $750 to repair, the red truck was $168 to repair, the black SUV was $2,654 to repair, and he also repaired a green convertible. How much did the green convertible cost to repair if Mark made $8,617.26?

(A) Mark charged the owner of the green convertible $4,960.26 to repair the damage.

(B) Mark charged the owner of the green convertible $3,657 to repair the damage.

(C) Mark charged the owner of the green convertible $2,654 to repair the damage.

(D) Mark charged the owner of the green convertible $4,690.26 to repair the damage.

(29)   What numerical expression shows five hundred twenty to the third power increased by two hundred and nine?

(A) $520^3 \times 209$

(B) $520^3 + 209$

(C) $520 \times 3 + 209$

(D) $520 \times 3 \times 209$

(30)   Mark is replacing the floors in his living room. The flooring is $2.75 a square foot. If the room is 14 feet by 14 feet, how much will it cost to buy the flooring he needs?

(A)   To replace the floors in his living room, it will cost Mark $38.50.

(B)   To replace the floors in his living room, it will cost Mark $539.

(C)   To replace the floors in his living room, it will cost Mark $538.

(D)   To replace the floors in his living room, it will cost Mark $196.

Test 4 Essay Question

Unlike the other portions of your practice test, there is no right or wrong answer for your essay, so this portion of your practice test will not have an answer section.

Essay Topic

Your imagination is a beautiful part of your mind. If you could imagine your perfect home, what would it look like, where would it be located and what kind of weather would there be?

Test 4 Answers – Verbal Reasoning

In this Practice Test Answer Key, you will find the correct answer for each of the questions on Practice Test 4. The correct answer will be followed by an explanation to clarify why that answer is correct.

Test 4 Synonyms – Answers

(1)   The correct answer is: **D) obscured** – unclear, murky or difficult to understand.

HAZY – meaning muddled, unclear and obscured. The answer that means similar to HAZY is **obscured.**

(2)   The correct answer is: **A) incompetent** – meaning ineffective, hopeless or not up to a task.

INEPT – useless, bungled or ham-fisted. The answer that means similar to INEPT is **incompetent**.

(3)   The correct answer is: **B) euphoria** – excitement, joyous and elation.

JUBILATION – very happy, joyous or delighted. The answer that has the closest meaning to JUBILATION is **euphoria.**

(4)   The correct answer is: **C) flexibility** – to give or allow extra space.

LEEWAY – freedom, latitude or breathing room. The answer that has the closest meaning to LEEWAY is **flexibility.**

(5)   The correct answer is: **D) wayward** – disobedient, defiant or rebellious.

MISCHIEF – trouble, tomfoolery and naughtiness. The answer that has the closest meaning to MISCHIEF is **wayward.**

(6)   The correct answer is: **A) flippant** – offhanded, glib or dismissive.

NONCHALANT – casual, blasé or laidback. The answer that has the closest meaning to NONCHALANT is **flippant.**

(7)   The correct answer is: **B) infinite** – goes on forever.

OMNISCIENT – all-knowing. The answer that has the closest meaning to OMNISCIENT is **infinite.**

(8)   The correct answer is: **C) fossilize** – harden, solidify or set.

PETRIFY – turn to stone, solidify or alarm. The answer that has the closest meaning to PETRIFY is **fossilize.**

(9)   The correct answer is: **D) averse** – unenthusiastic, disinclined or reluctant.

RELUCTANT – unwilling, hesitant, unenthusiastic. The answer that has the closest meaning to RELUCTANT is **averse.**

(10)   The correct answer is: **A) lethargic** – lazy, weary or exhausted.

SLUGGISH – slow to react, tired or lethargic. The answer that has the closest meaning to SLUGGISH is **lethargic.**

(11)   The correct answer is: **B) topography** – geography, landscape or scenery.

TERRAIN – land, landscape or environment. The answer that has the closest meaning to TERRAIN is **topography.**

(12)   The correct answer is: **C) metropolitan** – municipal, urban or inner-city.

URBAN – city. The answer that has the closest meaning to URBAN is **metropolitan.**

(13)   The correct answer is: **D) vibrant** – bubbly, bright or animated.

VIVID – clear, bright. The answer that has the closest meaning to VIVID is **vibrant.**

(14)   The correct answer is: **A) hero** – conqueror, champion or brave individual.

PROTAGONIST – the main character, leading role or hero. The answer that has the closest meaning to PROTAGONIST is **hero.**

(15)   The correct answer is: **B) initiate** – instigate, instruct, and begin.

ORIGINATE – start off, begin, invent or come from. The answer that has the closest meaning to ORIGINATE is **initiate.**

(16)   The correct answer is: **C) striking** – unusual, prominent and remarkable.

CONSPICUOUS – obvious, evident or in plain sight. The answer that has the closest meaning to CONSPICUOUS is **striking.**

(17)   The correct answer is: **D) govern** – to reign, manage or preside over.

DOMINATE – to control, lead or rule. The answer that has the closest meaning to DOMINATE is **govern.**

Test 4 Sentence Completion – Answers

(1)   The correct answer is: **C) disintegrate**

My paper chain decorations hanging from the tree began to **disintegrate** in the rain.

EXPLANATION: Disintegrate means to fall apart. The paper chain outside began to fall apart in the rain.

(2)   The correct answer is: **D) immersing**

Diving on the coral reef was like **immersing** myself into a whole new world.

EXPLANATION: Immersing means to sink into something completely. So diving on the coral reef was like entering a different world.

(3)   The correct answer is: **A) linger**

By the time I left work, it was getting dark and I didn't want to **linger.**

EXPLANATION: Linger means to hang around. It was getting dark when they got off work so they didn't want to hang around; they wanted to get home.

(4)   The correct answer is: **A) the next play to win the game.**

I joined the huddle as we chose **the next play to win the game.**

EXPLANATION: Based on the context of the sentence, you want to choose the most positive action possible in order to win the game. Answer B, "outrageous thing" and answer D, "least likely to win," therefore do not make sense. Answer C, "best score," just doesn't fit.

(5)   The correct answer is: **C) route**

The best **route** home is through the park, past the bakery and over the creek.

EXPLANATION: Answer D doesn't fit the sentence at all; trail and road refer to the type of path but are not the best way to get home. The **route** is the only word that refers to the actual path and way to get home.

(6)   The correct answer is: **D) vacate**

It's time to **vacate** this horrible place and find a more suitable home.

EXPLANATION: Answers A, B and C all refer to staying in place. D is the only option that means to leave.

(7)   The correct answer is: **B) vital**

Water is **vital** to the survival of the human body.

EXPLANATION: The other answers mean "unimportant" and "inferior" This sentence is talking about the importance of something to your body. Therefore, **vital** is the only logical answer.

(8)   The correct answer is: **C) alternate**

QUESTION: The dress I have chosen for the emperor's arrival will **alternate** between the colors of blue and gold.

EXPLANATION: Alternate means to fluctuate.

(9)   The correct answer is: **A) food and treats.**

The banquet for the jubilee will be full of delicious **food and treats.**

EXPLANATION: The sentence is referring to the taste of something. Options B, C and D refer to things you can't eat or taste.

(10)   The correct answer is: **D) character**

The strength of your **character** goes a long way to show the kind of person you are.

EXPLANATION: Character refers to how someone acts and treats others.

(11)   The correct answer is: **A) document**

The document needs to be signed in order to close the purchase of the new house.

EXPLANATION: Options B and C are types of documents but don't fit the sentence as well as document. Answer B, investment, is not something you would sign.

(12)   The correct answer is: **B) perish**

The world will **perish** if we allow hatred to tear us apart.

EXPLANATION: Options A, C and D refer to rising or growing. If the world will be torn apart from hatred it will die or perish, not grow or do well.

(13)   The correct answer is: **C) oasis**

I want to create an **oasis** for my relaxation and enjoyment.

EXPLANATION: Oasis refers to a place to relax. An aviary is for birds, a corral is for horses and a penitentiary is a prison or jail. None of those make a good place to relax and enjoy yourself.

(14)   The correct answer is: **D) inept**

My father's accountant is a loathsome, **inept** little man who often makes messes of things.

EXPLANATION: A, B and C are all pleasant and positive actions. **Inept** means to be incompetent or unable to do things. Therefore, if the accountant is loathsome and messes things up, he can't be positive or helpful.

(15)   The correct answer is: **A) constant**

My best friend David is my **constant** companion and only confidant.

EXPLANATION: Answers B, C and D refer to being rude, unhelpful or inferior. Therefore, **constant,** meaning steadfast and loyal, is the best description of the type of friend David is.

(16)   The correct answer is: **B) domesticated**

A wolf pup was found on our doorstep last year. Surprisingly, he has become quite **domesticated.**

EXPLANATION: Answers A, C and D are behaviors you would most likely expect from a wild animal. However, for a wolf to be domesticated would be surprising.

(17)   The correct answer is: **C) I was sorry to have to say bye.**

I had a wonderful time at Grandpa's house and **was sorry to have to say bye.**

EXPLANATION: Buy means to purchase, **by** refers to location, but **bye** means to leave or wish farewell. So the spelling **bye** is the best fit for this sentence.

Test 4 Answers – Quantitative Reasoning

(1)   The correct answer is: **C) (4 × 2) 6 = number of blocks run in six days.**

Explanation: If 4 miles is run 2 times a day, that can be represented as (4 × 2). The runner runs that same amount for 6 days, which would be (4 × 2) 6. Or a total of 48 miles in the six days.

(2)   The correct answer is: **B) Divide the total cost by 20 cents to find the total weight of the packages sent. Then take the total weight in pounds and subtract the weights of packages A, B and C. This will give you the weight of package D by elimination.**

(3)   The correct answer is: **B) Gallons**

(4)   The correct answer is: **C) Column B – Students who take the bus.**

(5)   The correct answer is: **C) Aaron's A-framed house is shaped like a triangle.**

(6)   The correct answer is: **C) Fluid ounces**

(7)   The correct answer is: **A) $9^3 = 729$**

(8)   The correct answer is: **D) the average of a set of numbers**

(9)   The correct answer is: **A) Becky and Trish are 28 years old.**

Explanation: If Becky and Trish have a combined age of 56, and Becky and Trish are the same age, then we can just take the total (56) and divide it by 2. This makes both Becky and Trish 28 years old.

(10)   The correct answer is: **D) Hundred thousands**

(11)   The correct answer is: **C) Mixed number**

(12)   The correct answer is: **B) Cubed**

(13)   The correct answer is: **A) All three turtles are moving a foot per minute.**

Explanation: The first turtle is moving 1 ft/min, which is given. The second turtle is moving 12 in/min, which when converted is 1 ft/min (12 in = 1 ft). The third turtle is moving at 30.48 cm/min, which when converted is 1 ft/min (30.48 cm = 1 ft). Therefore, although their speeds are represented with different units, they all represent 1 ft/min.

(14)   The correct answer is: **A) -20**

Explanation: When looking at the values and considering the distance from one, Answer A) -20 is a distance of 21 from 1. Answer B) 20 is only a distance of 19 from 1. Answer C) 0 is only a distance of 1 from 1, and Answer D) 15 is a distance of 14 from 1. Therefore, the number furthest from 1 is A) -20.

(15)   The correct answer is: **D) 25% of your supply order is on back-order.**

(16)   The correct answer is: **C) The GCF of 3, 9, 12 and 18 is 3.**

(17)   The correct answer is: **D) The LCM of 12, 24, 36 and 48 is 144.**

(18)   The correct answer is: **A) The LCM of 100, 400 and 800 is 800.**

(19)　The correct answer is: **D) The factors of 111 in lowest terms are 37 and 3.**

(20)　The correct answer is: **B) 193**

Explanation: When looking for a prime number, you are looking for a number that only one and itself go into. If you look at the answer choices for A, C, and D, they all are divisible by 1, 2, and the given number, thus not prime. 193 is the only prime number given.

(21)　The correct answer is: **C) Myles drives about 14 miles per hour.**

(22)　The correct answer is: **A) 980 is a multiple of 49.**

(23)　The correct answer is: **D) 12×10^{-9}**

(24)　The correct answer is: **B) The LCD of this set of fractions is 12.**

(25)　The correct answer is: **D) Micah needs to order 34 items.**

(26)　The correct answer is: **B) Educational Taxes make up 17% of the city's revenue.**

Explanation: Given the total revenue is represented by 100%, subtract off each of the given categories, and whatever is left will be the percent for Educational Taxes.

100% − 9% (Sales Tax) − 42% (Gift Tax) − 32% (DMV Fees) = 17% (Educational Taxes).

(27)   The correct answer is: **B) Anna's haircut cost \$32.**

(28)   The correct answer is: **C) Mavis needs about 2 bushels of peaches.**

(29)   The correct answer is: **D) Melissa will need 24 bags of chocolate chips.**

(30)   The correct answer is: **B) Each archer will have 5 chances to score a bull's-eye from each position.**

(31)   The correct answer is: **A) *x* is greater than fifty-six.**

(32)   The correct answer is: **C) A whole number**

(33)   The correct answer is: **D) The mural is most likely a square.**

(34)   The correct answer is: **C) The doorway has to be at least 4 feet wide.**

(35)   The correct answer is: **A) Lynne is 48, Mary is 52 and Debbie is 58.**

Explanation: If Amy is 36 and Lynne is 12 years older than Amy, Lynne is 48. If Mary is 4 years older than Lynne, than Mary is 52. Finally, if Debbie is 6 years older than Mary, then Debbie is 58.

(36)   The correct answer is: **B) A is 30 degrees, B is 70 degrees and C is 40 degrees.**

(37)   The correct answer is: **A) The large leak buckets at 9 p.m., the medium leak bucket at 11 p.m. and the small leak buckets at 2 a.m.**

(38)   The correct answer is: **B) There are 50 of each color jelly bean in the jar.**

Test 4 Answers – Reading Comprehension

Test 4 Passage 1 – Answers

This passage is about the speech that Richard Nixon gave to defend himself while running for vice president of the United States. The speech he gave later became known as the "Checkers" speech.

(1)   The correct answer is: **D) All of the above. Nixon gave his Checkers speech to defend himself, prove he had done nothing wrong and to be transparent with the American people**

QUESTION: Why did Richard Nixon feel the need to give his Checkers Speech?

EXPLANATION: The answer to this question can be found in lines 11-20 of this passage: "He defended himself, saying he had never misused funds or given special favors to anyone, and he never would. His benefactors would never be given anything he wouldn't give to any other constituents. He continued by saying his government stipend only covered very specific things related to his office and not his political career. He added that it would be morally wrong to charge the taxpayers for any of those expenses and said all the money in the fund had been used to pay for expenses in his political career. Then, he was transparent about his personal finances. He went after his opponents, saying they should also give a full accounting of their finances, as well as pointing out some of the shady things he felt some Democrats were doing."

(2)   The correct answer is: **B) Richard Nixon was running for vice president of the United States.**

QUESTION: What role was Nixon trying to obtain at the time of the speech?

EXPLANATION: The answer to this question can be found in lines 3, 26 and 28 of this passage: "He had been announced two months earlier as Dwight D. Eisenhower's running mate ... Following the speech, the American people rallied behind Nixon ... all of which supported Nixon and ensured his spot on the ticket as vice president."

(3)   The correct answer is: **A) The American people supported Nixon.**

QUESTION: Following the speech, what was the reaction of the American people?

EXPLANATION: The answer to this question can be found in line 26: "Following the speech, the American people rallied behind Nixon."

(4)   The correct answer is: **B) Checkers was the black and white family dog.**

QUESTION: Who was Checkers?

EXPLANATION: The answer to this question can be found in lines 24-25: "He told the public that regardless of how things turned out, the one gift he wouldn't give back was a black and white dog his kids loved and called Checkers."

(5)   The correct answer is: **C) September 23, 1953, in L.A.**

QUESTION: Where and when did Richard Nixon deliver his Checkers speech?

EXPLANATION: The answer to this question can be found in lines 1-2 and 7: "On September 23, 1953, California senator Richard Nixon gave a televised speech to the American people ... Richard Nixon left his West Coast tour and flew to L.A. to make his speech."

Test 4 Passage 2 – Answers

This passage is about World War II, how the war broke out in the first place, the events that took place during the war and the actions that finally ended the war.

(1)   The correct answer is: **D) The German invasion of Poland is considered the catalyst that started World War II.**

QUESTION: What landmark event is considered to have started World War II?

EXPLANATION: The answer to this question can be found in lines 3-4: "though the landmark start of World War II was September 1, 1939, when Germany invaded Poland."

(2)   The correct answer is: **C) The two sides of World War II were the Allies and the Axis.**

QUESTION: What were the two sides in WWII called?

EXPLANATION: The answer to this question can be found in line 19. Also, lines 19-23 provide an explanation: "WWII was split into two sides: the Allies and the Axis. The Axis was made up of Germany, Italy and Japan. The Allies were comprised of Great Britain, France and the United States. To the surprise of many, the Soviet Union also joined the Allies, after Germany broke its non-aggression pact and invaded the Soviet Union."

(3)   The correct answer is: **B) The atomic bomb was used to ultimately end the war.**

QUESTION: What weapon was used to ultimately end WWII? **EXPLANATION:** The answer to this question can be found in lines 30-38: "After land losses to Japan, it was decided that a land attack risked too many lives. Instead, the decision was made to use the atomic Bomb. The A-bomb was only ever used twice. The first time it was used was on August 6, 1945, in the bombing of Hiroshima. The bomb was delivered by a B-29 bomber plane. When the Japanese didn't surrender right away, a second A-bomb was used in the bombing of Nagasaki three days later on August 9, 1945. The results were so devastating that the Japanese emperor surrendered over a radio broadcast on August 15, 1945, finally ending World War II."

(4)   The correct answer is: **C) Adolf Hitler is considered to be the instigator of World War II.**

QUESTION: What major leader started WWII?

EXPLANATION: The answer to this question can be found in lines 5-7: "World War II was a joint effort by Germany and the Soviet Union. Adolf Hitler and Joseph Stalin signed a non-aggression pact in August 1939. The idea was Hitler's. He wanted to grow a German race that would rival all others."

(5)   The correct answer is: **B) Hitler wanted to make room to grow his Aryan race.**

QUESTION: Why did the Germans go to war?

EXPLANATION: The answer can be found in lines 7-9: "The idea was Hitler's. He wanted to grow a German race that would rival all others. He dubbed it the Aryan race and the war was meant to clear out the 'trash' in order to make room for his Aryan race to grow and thrive."

Test 4 Passage 3 – Answers

This passage is a poem about a schoolhouse. Many of the answers in this passage will be based on descriptive language and imagery, with more implied content than things which are said outright.

(1)   The correct answer is: **A) The poem is talking about a schoolhouse.**

QUESTION: What is the place the poem is talking about?

EXPLANATION: The answer to this question can logically be concluded from lines 1-3: "A building covered in bright red lacquer, trimmed in a striking white. A golden bell upon the steeple ringing out to signal the start of our day. Desks and chairs sit quietly as pupils file in evenly." The building is red, with a bell that rings to tell students it's time to go inside. Based on those three lines, the inference can easily be made that this is a school.

(2)   The correct answer is: **B) A teacher.**

QUESTION: Who is the "she" and "her" in the poem referring to?

EXPLANATION: The answer to the question can be logically concluded based on lines 4-6 and 8: "Her heels click along the wood planks. The chalk dancing across the board ahead, clicking along the path it makes. A beautiful scroll of knowledge she writes ... She rings the brass bell upon her desk when it's time to take our lunch." Those lines should make it very easy to discern that "she" is in front of the class at the chalkboard, teaching, and the fact that she is the one to ring the bell on her desk implies that she is important enough to tell the class when they can go out for lunch. Both lead to a logical conclusion that "she" and "her" refer to a teacher.

(3)   The correct answer is: **C) The bell in the steeple is gold.**

QUESTION: What color is the bell in the steeple?

EXPLANATION: The answer to this question can be found in line 2: "A golden bell upon the steeple ringing out to signal the start of our day."

(4)   The correct answer is: **D) The trim on the schoolhouse is white.**

QUESTION: What color is the trim of the schoolhouse?

EXPLANATION: The answer to this question can be found in line 1 of this poem: "A building covered in bright red lacquer, trimmed in a striking white."

(5)   The correct answer is: **B) At the end of the day, the pupils go home.**

QUESTION: Where do the pupils go when the bell rings at the end of the day?

EXPLANATION: The answer to this question can be found in lines 13-15: "Time to find our way back home. To a warm embrace in our mother's home. To cozy beds where we close our day."

Test 4 Passage 4 – Answers

This passage is a poem about fishing. The poem is very descriptive and paints a visual picture of the surroundings and the activities taking place. The answers in this passage have more to do with what you read and infer rather than from facts pulled right out of the text.

(1)   The correct answer is: **B) The poem is about fishing.**

QUESTION: What is the poem about?

EXPLANATION: The answer to this question can be found in lines 1, 3, 5, 6 and 11 of this poem: "We stroll along the water's edge … The water shallow, the sun is hot … A hook concealed by a wormy treat. My bobber floats along lazily … Soon I pull up a big fat bass." While the poem doesn't specifically say fishing, it is a logical conclusion based on the description provided.

(2)   The correct answer is: **C) In the poem, the hook is concealed by a wormy treat.**

QUESTION: What conceals the hook in the poem?

EXPLANATION: The answer to this question can be found in line 5: "A hook concealed by a wormy treat."

(3)   The correct answer is: **A) The scales on the fish are slippery.**

QUESTION: What word describes the scales?

EXPLANATION: The answer to this question can be found in line 12: "Slippery scales slide in my hand."

(4)   The correct answer is: **D) All of the above.**

QUESTION: Where are they fishing?

EXPLANATION: The answers to this question can be found in lines 1-4: "We stroll along the water's edge. Fallen trees and reeds they're home. The water shallow, the sun is hot. The perfect weather for their habitat." Those four lines describe shallow water, reeds and trees, and the water's edge, all implying that they are fishing near the shore among reeds and trees.

(5)   The correct answer is: **A) The poem says that the warm and shallow water make the perfect habitat.**

QUESTION: What makes the perfect habitat?

EXPLANATION: The answer to this question can be found in lines 3-4: "The water shallow, the sun is hot. The perfect weather for their habitat."

Test 4 Passage 5 – Answers

This passage is about the country of Scotland, when it was founded, a brief history and where the country stands today.

(1) The correct answer is: **C) Scotland was formed in the early middle ages.**

QUESTION: When was Scotland formed?

EXPLANATION: The answer to this question can be found in lines 1-2: "Scotland is part of the United Kingdom now, but when it was formed in the early middle ages it was its own country."

(2) The correct answer is: **B) King James VI**

QUESTION: Who joined Scotland with the United Kingdom?

EXPLANATION: The answer can be found in lines 6-10: "King James VI was the closest relative to inherit the throne, thus becoming King James I of England and Ireland in addition to his title of King James VI of Scotland. That inheritance joined the three countries together. King James VI joined the countries politically on May 1, 1707."

(3) The correct answer is: **A) Great Britain and Scotland share the southeastern Scottish border.**

QUESTION: What border do Great Britain and Scotland share?

EXPLANATION: The answer to this question can be found in line 19: "It borders the United Kingdom along the southeast."

(4) The correct answer is: **C) The capital of Scotland is Edinburgh.**

QUESTION: What is the capital of Scotland?

EXPLANATION: The answer to this question can be found in lines 23-24: "While Scotland is well known for the city of Inverness and the Loch Ness Monster, its capital city is actually Edinburgh."

(5)   The correct answer is: **D) Scotland is bordered on three sides by water.**

QUESTION: What borders Scotland on three sides?

EXPLANATION: The answer to this question can be found in lines 19-20: "It borders the United Kingdom along the southeast. It is surrounded by water on all other sides."

Test 4 Mathematics Achievement

(1)   The correct answer is: **C) Mary would have 258 gumballs left after 14 days.**

EXPLANATION: Mary took 1 gumball every day and an extra 2 on Friday (so she took 3 on Fridays). Starting on a Monday means she would have taken 9 gumballs every seven days, so in 14 days she would have taken 18 gumballs. Subtract 18 from the total number of gumballs in the jar when she started to get the correct answer. 276 − 18 = 258 gumballs left.

(2)   The correct answer is: **A) The trip from America to Germany is 4,898 miles.**

EXPLANATION: Johan's whole trip is 10,917 miles. To find the missing miles for the trip from America back to Germany, subtract the values you have from the total miles traveled: 10,917 − 650 = 10,267 − 5,369 = 4,898. Check all three trip distances sum together to the correct amount: 650 + 5,369 + 4,898 = 10,917.

(3)   The correct answer is: **B) The square root of 169 is 13.**

EXPLANATION: The symbol $\sqrt{}$ means square root. The question is asking what the square root of 169 is. The factor that multiplies by itself to give 169 is 13. To check the answer, multiply the answer by itself to ensure it matches your answer. $13 \times 13 = 169$. Therefore, the square root of 169 is 13.

(4)   The correct answer is: **B) The square root of 289 is 17.**

EXPLANATION: The square root of 289 is 17. Multiply 17 by itself to ensure you get the correct answer.

(5)   The correct answer is: **D) The area of the triangle is 35 square inches**.

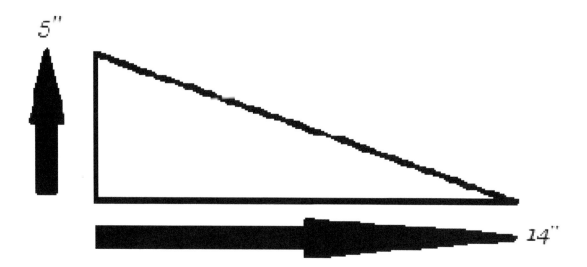

EXPLANATION: The area of a triangle formula is A=1/2(bh). Therefore, to find the area of a triangle you multiply the width of the triangle by the height of the triangle and divide the product by two. In this case, the triangle is 5 inches high and 14 inches wide. 5 × 14 = 70. Then you divide that 70 by 2 and get the answer 35. Therefore, the area of the triangle is 35 inches squared.

(6)   The correct answer is: **B) The square root of 100 is 10.**

EXPLANATION: To find the square root of 100, find a factor of 100 which multiplies by itself to give 100. 10 × 10 = 100. Therefore, the square root of 100 is 10.

(7)   The correct answer is: **C) 407,690.**

(8)   The correct answer is: **C) 125^5.**

(9)   The correct answer is: **A) 21^3.**

(10)   The correct answer is: **A) 500,652,800.50.**

(11)   The correct answer is: **C) The GCF of 120, 160 and 220 is 20.**

EXPLANATION: The Greatest Common Factor or GCF of all three numbers 120, 160 and 220 is 20.

(12)   The correct answer is: **B) Ten millions.**

EXPLANATION: The number is 562,408,000.70 in numeric form. The number 6 is in the ten millions place.

(13)   The correct answer is: **D) 28% of the students are in pottery class.**

EXPLANATION: Percentages are out of 100. If you deduct the percentage values from 100, you will find the answer. 100 − 42 = 58 − 13 = 45 − 17 = 28. Therefore, 28% of the students are in pottery class.

(14)   The correct answer is: **A) 20% haven't RSVP'd for the party yet.**

EXPLANATION: To find the percentage for this equation you will divide 100 by the total number of guests invited to get each person's percentage value (100 ÷ 25 = 4). Each party guest represents 4% of the whole group. If 20 people have sent their RSVP, multiply the number of RSVPs received by the 4% that represents the guests (20 × 4 = 80). Therefore, 80% of the guests have sent their RSVPs, which means 20% haven't RSVP'd for the party yet.

(15)   The correct answer is: **B) 4 + 5 > 4 − 5.**

EXPLANATION: 4 + 5 = 9, 4 − 5 = -1. The symbol > means greater than. Therefore, 4 + 5 is greater than 4 − 5 (4 + 5 > 4 − 5).

(16)   The correct answer is: **C) 4 × 12 ≤ 12 × 4.**

EXPLANATION: For this statement, the sum of each side of the inequality are is the same. The symbol representing less than or equal to is ≤ . Therefore, answer C correctly answers the question.

(17)   The correct answer is: **A) Sarah runs 36 miles each week.**

EXPLANATION: Sarah runs 6 miles twice a week and 8 miles three times a week. So Sarah runs five days a week. To find the total miles Sarah runs, multiply six miles by two days and then eight miles by three days: 6 × 2 = 12, 8 × 3 = 24. Then find the total: 12 + 24 = 36 miles.

(18)   The correct answer is: **B) x = 9.**

EXPLANATION: To solve for x, work the problem in reverse to find the missing value of x. 112 − 13 = 99 ; 99 ÷ 11 = 9. The value of x is 9.

(19)   The correct answer is: **A) 74.**

EXPLANATION: Using the values provided, solve the equation. b = 49, a = 12, c = 37. Solve the equation 49 − 12 = 37 ; 37 + 37 = 74. Therefore, the solution to the equation is 74.

(20)   The correct answer is: **A) Lucy's total bill for lunch with Kevin's 20% tip will be $65.45.**

EXPLANATION: 20% of $54.54 is $10.91. So the total cost of the meal with the tip added on is $54.54 + $10.91 = $65.45.

(21)   The correct answer is: **B) 4,599,000.**

EXPLANATION: The word problem is asking you to round to the nearest thousand. The thousands place is the fourth place value to the left of the decimal point. The first number to the right of the place value you are rounding tells you which way to round it. Numbers 1 through 4 round down and numbers 5 through 9 round up. Since there is a 6 on the right of the 8, we round up. Therefore, the number 4,598,632 rounded to the nearest thousand is 4,599,000.

(22)   The correct answer is: **A) 300,000,000 + 4,000,000 + 600,000 + 80,000 + 9,000 + 900 + 80 + 7.**

EXPLANATION: Expanded form is separating the number out by each place value. Therefore, 304,689,987 is correctly expressed in expanded form in answer A.

(23)   The correct answer is: **C) 1,671,392**

EXPLANATION: 1,598,147 + 69,248 = 1,667,395 + 3,997 = 1,671,392

(24)   The correct answer is: **C) 114**

EXPLANATION: To solve the equation start with the numbers in parentheses: (6×6) = 36. Work the equation with the solved value of the numbers in parentheses. $14 \div 7 \times 36 + 42 = ?$ $14 \div 7 = 2 \times 36 = 72 + 42 = 114$. Therefore, the correct answer is 114.

(25)   The correct answer is: **D) 87,001,000**

(26)   The correct answer is: **B) Hundred thousands**

EXPLANATION: The numerical form of the word problem is 1,756,020. The number 7 is in the hundred thousands place.

(27)   The correct answer is: **C) The boys ran a total of 144 miles.**

EXPLANATION: The boys run 6 miles a day, 6 days a week, for 4 weeks. To solve the problem, multiply 6 miles by 6 days a week which will give you the number of miles run in a week. Multiply the weekly miles by the 4 weeks they are training to get the total miles.

$(6 \times 6) \times 4$ = total training miles. $6 \times 6 = 36 \times 4 = 144$ miles.

(28)   The correct answer is: **A) Mark charged the owner of the green convertible $4,960.26 to repair the damage.**

EXPLANATION: To solve the equation you will use the information to find the missing value. Mark earned a total of $8,617.26 for the whole week. Deduct the two oil changes and the cost of the three repairs from the total earned for the week to find the value of the green convertible repairs.

$8,617.26 – ($42.50 \times 2) – $750 – $168 – $2,654 =

$8,617.26 – $85 = $8,532.26

$8,532.26 –$750.00 = $7782.26

$7,782.26 – $168.00 = $7,614.26

$7,614.26 – $2,654.00 = $4,960.26.

(29)   The correct answer is: **B) $520^3 + 209$**

(30)   The correct answer is: **B) To replace the floors in his living room, it will cost Mark $539.**

EXPLANATION: Solve the problem by finding the area of the room and then multiply it by the cost of the flooring per square foot. The room is 14 feet by 14 feet (14 × 14 = 196). The area of the room is 196 square feet. Now take the area of the room and multiply it by the cost of flooring per square foot (196 × $2.75 = $539). Therefore, it will cost $539 to replace the flooring.

Conclusion

This is the end of this test preparation book. Our team hopes you received enough practice by solving the practice questions in this study guide. Good luck!

CPSIA information can be obtained
at www.ICGtesting.com
Printed in the USA
LVHW021424300820
664580LV00001B/375